COMMUNAL SOCIETIES IN AMERICA
AN AMS REPRINT SERIES

RELIGIOUS FANATICISM

AMS PRESS
NEW YORK

RELIGIOUS FANATICISM

EXTRACTS FROM THE PAPERS OF
HANNAH WHITALL SMITH

EDITED
WITH AN INTRODUCTION BY

RAY STRACHEY

CONSISTING OF AN ACCOUNT OF THE AUTHOR OF
THESE PAPERS, AND OF THE TIMES IN WHICH SHE
LIVED ; TOGETHER WITH A DESCRIPTION OF
THE CURIOUS RELIGIOUS SECTS AND
COMMUNITIES OF AMERICA DURING
THE EARLY AND MIDDLE YEARS
OF THE NINETEENTH
CENTURY

LONDON
Faber & Gwyer Limited
24 Russell Square W.C.1

Library of Congress Cataloging in Publication Data

Smith, Hannah Whitall, 1832-1911.
    Religious fanaticism.

    (Communal societies in America)
    Reprint of the 1928 ed. published by Faber & Gwyer, London.
    Includes index.
    1. Sects — United States. 2. Fanaticism. 3. Smith, Hannah
Whitall, 1832-1911. I. Title.
BR516.5.S55 1976   280'.0973   72-8252
ISBN 0-404-11005-3

Reprinted from an original copy in the collections
of the University of Chicago Library

From the edition of 1928, London
First AMS edition published in 1976
Manufactured in the United States of America

AMS PRESS INC.
NEW YORK, N.Y.

PREFACE

My Grandmother's papers here published, and the documents and books from which my own introduction is drawn, are the sources upon which my novel, 'Shaken by the Wind', was founded. It was difficult in the novel, and has been still more difficult here to write impartially about the queer beliefs and practices of religious and reforming cranks. One is tempted to condemn them as wicked, to mock at them as absurd, or to pity them as mad ; and they do undoubtedly display symptoms to justify all these comments.

I do not believe, however, that a complete description can be made up of these elements alone. Psycho-analysis certainly reveals how sex and religion can be intertwined in abnormal sects, and resolves some of their contradictions, and historical research puts them into perspective, and shows that they were not peculiar to one continent or century. Neither psycho-analysis nor history, however, can explain the impulse which drove the false prophets out into their fantastic and erotic search for truth : and until we understand their motives we cannot fully judge them.

In my Grandmother's generation the motive was thought to be the devil, but I have not made that assumption. I have tried instead, both in this book and in the novel, to tell the story plainly and without bias, leaving the facts to speak for themselves.

RAY STRACHEY

Cavalière, 1928.

v

CONTENTS

INTRODUCTION

BY RAY STRACHEY

AN ACCOUNT OF THE AUTHOR OF THESE PAPERS, AND OF THE TIMES IN WHICH SHE LIVED ; TOGETHER WITH A DESCRIPTION OF THE CURIOUS RELIGIOUS SECTS AND COMMUNITIES OF AMERICA DURING THE EARLY AND MIDDLE YEARS OF THE NINETEENTH CENTURY

CONTENTS

PERSONAL EXPERIENCES OF RELIGIOUS FANATICISM
BY HANNAH WHITALL SMITH

INTRODUCTION

AN ACCOUNT OF THE AUTHOR OF THESE PAPERS, AND OF
THE TIMES IN WHICH SHE LIVED ; TOGETHER WITH A
DESCRIPTION OF THE CURIOUS RELIGIOUS SECTS AND
COMMUNITIES OF AMERICA DURING THE EARLY AND
MIDDLE YEARS OF THE NINETEENTH CENTURY.

BY RAY STRACHEY

CHAPTER I

HANNAH WHITALL SMITH

HANNAH WHITALL SMITH, the author of the Personal Experiences which follow, was born in Philadelphia in 1832, a birthright member of the Society of Friends. The great interest of her life was her search for religious truth, and in the course of this great adventure she wandered into strange places and met with strange men. Always, from first to last, she looked for good rather than evil, and believed that something of value might be anywhere revealed. She approached all creeds and all believers in a perfectly simple and straightforward hope that the Lord might be speaking through them, and although her hope was constantly frustrated and her trust continually shaken, she never lost her conviction that the false prophets and the wild cranks of her acquaintance were more mistaken than wicked, more deluded than deliberately deceitful.

It was in consequence of this attitude of mind that so many strange secrets were confided to her ; and, as she was not only sympathetic, but also exceedingly vigorous, her explorations covered a wide field.

An outline of the facts of her life will give some idea of her standing in the religious world, and, although no description can properly convey the vigorous quality of her nature, something of her attitude of mind will be revealed in her own papers, which are here published for the first time.

Hannah Whitall was brought up amid the restrictions and limitations of the Quakers of the middle of the last century. She was taught that it was wrong to live as the worldly lived, to dress or speak as they did, or to mingle with their affairs. Art and music were ' gay ' and sinful, and fiction was a snare of the devil. Day dreaming and wandering thoughts, whistling and even excessive laughter were temptations, and the true Christian was he who lived always in quietness and recollection.

To Hannah's vehement and exuberant nature this doctrine was hard ; and though she did her best to school herself to it, she was aware that she was not very successful. ' The laugh is in me,' she wrote in her diary, ' and it seems as if it must come out.'

At nineteen Hannah Whitall married Robert Pearsall Smith, also a Friend ; and with him her search for righteousness was carried out beyond the boundaries of the Quaker fold. Robert was as earnest as his wife, and as deeply convinced of the importance of the search for God ; and the two of them set off, after their marriage, upon a sort of religious exploration. First they tried to introduce reforms into the Society to which they belonged ; then they joined successively the Methodists, the Plymouth Brethren and the Baptists ; and then they set out as Evangelists themselves, to preach the Higher Life. Both of them were wonderfully successful preachers ; Robert of the eloquent, emotional sort, and Hannah more practical, more explicit and simple. In 1873 they worked in England, and led more than one great revival, and then Robert went on into Germany, where, in spite of the drawback of preaching through an interpreter, he had an enormous success. This work led to the Conferences gathered by Lord and Lady Mount Temple at Broadlands in 1873 and 1874, which in their turn led to vast undenominational gatherings at Oxford and at Brighton. People from all over Europe came to take part in the movement, and Robert and Hannah were at the very centre of it all. The doctrine they were preaching was not sectarian ; they led no exodus from any of the Churches, but taught only the need for the Higher Life and the quickening of the religious impulse.

Trouble and scandal arose, however, and Robert was accused of preaching a secret doctrine, and was discredited among his colleagues. Hannah stood by him firmly, but the result of it all was that they decided to return home to America, and to leave their work to others. It was during the period of the Higher Life Movement that Hannah wrote and published her most successful book, ' The Christian's Secret of a Happy Life '. This book had not only a phenomenal sale all through her lifetime, but also a vast influence. It was reissued again and again, and translated not only into all the major languages of the world, but even into obscure dialects of half-civilized tribes. From every part of the globe there came testimonies to the help and comfort which this book brought, and Hannah's position as a religious teacher was established.

After the end of their connection with the Higher Life Movement, Robert gave up preaching, but his wife continued, and from then until the end of her life she wrote and taught what she believed might be helpful to Christian seekers. Letters and visitors flocked in upon her in thousands, and to all who came she gave the best comfort and the best advice she could, telling people always to trust to the loving kindness of God, and not to be troubled or afraid.

As time went on, however, her interest in practical reforms increased, and she took a very prominent part in the foundation of the Women's Christian Temperance Movement in the United States, and also in the Women's Suffrage Movement. She felt that in these ways, as well as by more directly religious work, she was furthering the purposes of God ; and she threw herself into them with delight.

In 1886 the whole family returned to England again, and settled there permanently ; and Hannah took up at once the same sort of public and religious work that she had been doing at home. She became Honorary Secretary of the British Women's Temperance Union, and continued to write and publish religious books and tracts, and occasionally to preach. As she grew older, however, she withdrew from so much active work, and contented herself with looking on at the new ways of the rising generation, which she was always inclined to approve. She was so intensely radical by nature that the mere fact that a thing was new was enough to recommend it to her, and she often rejoiced to see the last of the methods and ideas she had herself originated, declaring that what the young people substituted was almost certain to be better.

Her religious views underwent a steady development all through her life ; and she has herself described the progress of them very delightfully in the book she called ' The Unselfishness of God : A Spiritual Autobiography.' She found that, after all her searching and all her experimenting, she had come back very close to the position of the old Quakers from which she had started, and in her later years she was more mystical, more quietist, and at the same time less positive than in her active days. ' I care very little for anyone's talk on the subject of God, my own or any other,' she said, ' and sometimes I think I shall have to stop preaching because of this. It seems to me as if it would be enough to say, " God is " and "Be good", and then all would be said. . . . The will of God has truly become the very passion of my heart. . . . For me there is no religious life possible but the mystic life . . . the only clue I have is, " the Lord reigneth, let the earth rejoice ".'

While she was living thus, quiet, and untroubled by doubts or difficulties, Hannah looked back on her past life, and on the storms and excitements of the religious search she had pursued. ' All the tempests in the various religious teapots around me do seem so far off, so young, so green, so petty ! I KNOW I was there once, but it must have been ages ago ! ' But it was not so very far behind. The seekers and enquirers were following her still, writing and coming daily to get her help and advice, and the problems they brought her were the old problems which she had faced in her earlier life. She set herself therefore to give what practical help she could, personally and by writing, and it was in the hope that others might learn from her own experience that she wrote her later books. It was in this same spirit that, between 1890 and 1900 she put together the Fanaticism Papers which are published here.

' You must not publish them until after I am dead,' she told her children, ' nor until all the people I mention are dead. But then I think they ought to be published. It won't hurt any of us when we're dead to have it all known, though it would cause a lot of trouble now. However, we shan't care once we've all got to Heaven. And I think these things ought to be known, for they are a snare to so many poor, innocent, earnest souls.'

The final impulse to write these things down came to her from the results of her investigations into the case of Laurence Oliphant, which shocked her more than any of the other strange things she had encountered. She pursued the investigations in no spirit of enmity, and with no wish to do him or his friends an injury, but with the feeling that some time or other a warning against that sort of delusion should be uttered.

The discoveries she made about his teachings are told in these papers, but her first meeting with Laurence Oliphant is described in a letter written in August, 1886.

' I went to Dorking—to meet Laurence Oliphant. He has been living in Palestine for several years, and

actually owns the Plain of Armageddon ! His wife
died lately, and he has come over to England on a
mission to propagate a sort of mystic spiritualism of a
most peculiar kind. It is set forth in a book he and his
wife wrote in partnership called " Sympneumata." . . .
After dinner Laurence Oliphant read us a long paper
about " IT and He " of which I could make neither
head nor tail ; but I gathered that " IT " meant the
Sympneumata. It sounded like pure unadulterated
trash ! The next morning, however, he unfolded his
ideas to me, and they were about as I tell you. I told
him of the dangers I saw in his teachings, and illustrated
what I had to say by an account of the fanaticisms to
which similar teaching had led a great many good
people in America ; but I might as well have talked to
the whirlwind. I am very glad, however, that I know
what his teachings really are, as I can warn people more
intelligently against them. It seems very sad to see
such a really bright and good man so deluded.'

Hannah Whitall Smith's interest in the ' dear saints '
did not cease with the writing of the story of their
aberrations. She followed all their careers, as well as
she could, and made a great collection of newspaper
cuttings and tracts and pamphlets showing their delusions. All these she put together in large bundles,
marking them on the outside in her beautiful copper-
plate handwriting, and storing them in a large wooden
chest. Some day, she thought, they might be useful ;
some day the warnings they contained might be made
manifest. 'Had we been warned', she wrote to one of her

old friends, ' what might we not have been spared ! . . . I shall leave the story of it all to my children, to do what they like with.'

Hannah Whitall Smith died in 1911, and for some years the wooden box remained unopened, and the Fanaticism Papers untouched. An attempt was made to secure their publication in 1916, but no publisher was willing to consider them, the subject being, as they said, too unpleasant, and the papers altogether too outspoken. As time went on, however, the value of plain speaking began to be more widely appreciated, and when the Papers were brought to light again in 1927 no such difficulty remained. It seemed, however, necessary to add to and supplement them, not only with a short biographical sketch of their author, but also with an account of the state of society in which she lived. Events have moved so rapidly since the World War, and society has, in so many respects, completely changed, that things which were well understood and taken for granted when the Papers were written are now forgotten and ignored. The following account of the sects and religious peculiarities of America in the early and middle part of the nineteenth century is thus prefixed to her story, as showing the background out of which her experiments and her experiences arose ; and in the hope that those who read it through will better understand how so intelligent and honest a woman could approach the subject of religious vagaries, and could meet wild and half crazy religious fanatics with so much faith, charity and hope.

As her Papers show, Hannah Whitall Smith sincerely believed, even after all her sad experiences, that the fanatics she knew were acting in good faith. Wild and wicked as they sometimes appeared, she thought them at least sincere, and held that Christian charity should enter into our judgments concerning them. Without faith it is almost impossible to be convincing, and unless they had been honestly trying to reach the state of mystical communion with God they could none of them, she thought, have been successful. The fact that many of them fell away from their ideals, and descended to trickeries and shams made no difference. The snares which beset a prophet are many ; divination, wonder working and mystification are easier than a holding fast to the narrow road ; and once embarked upon these things it is doubtless difficult not to rush headlong to ruin. But in the beginning, she believed, the false prophets, like the true saints, have sought to know God.

There is one other point which she would have wished brought forward in any introduction to her book, for it emphasises the intention with which she wrote ; and that is the fact that delusions, deceptions and religious manias continue to flourish to this day. The sects and aberrations of half a century ago seem wild and outrageous now, and well nigh incredible ; but they can be paralleled quite closely by modern examples. We shall not here describe anything of recent date, nor any creed which still finds adherents ; but we must remember that the story is not ended, and that the old mistakes and the old follies are living still.

The history of religious error is as old as that of mankind, though it is not quite so complex. There have been myriads of false prophets, and their followers have been legion. Every creed has had fantastic variants and the number of strange sects has been enormous ; for the human mind seems to love mystery, enchantment and excess. If the field of religious aberration is vast, however, and if the phenomena it presents are staggering, they are not in outline difficult to understand. For there is much similarity in the manifestations of different ages, and the same problems, and the same solutions recur again and again.

For our purposes we do not need to go back to the primitive religions, or to trace out those remnants of old beliefs which are to be met with in later creeds. We must indeed remember that the origins of the sects we are to consider lie far back in the beginning of religious thought, and that fanatics and seers have always played upon the credulity of simple people, and kept alive a succession of astonishing delusions upon the great subjects of life and death, good and evil. Never since men first became conscious of the passage of time has there been any lack of false prophets. Between the rivers of Mesopotamia and among the sands of Egypt, as well as in the Tibetan hills and the dark African forests, strange esoteric sects have had their rise, and wild faiths and mystic orgies have been known. In every race and in every age the same impulses have arisen, the same experiments have been tried, and the same strange answers found for the impenetrable problems of existence. The forms have differed, but the essence has been the same ; for religious mania takes its rise in some of the deepest impulses of human nature, and finds its expression through some of the commonest of human failings.

For the purpose of understanding the American sects of the nineteenth century we need not travel back so far. It is enough to trace their ideas through the Christian era to see that their leaders did not stand alone, but were really following along well-made paths, and wrestling, in their new and unsophisticated world, with the very same problems which had tormented devout men and women in the first centuries after Christ, had maddened them in the Middle Ages, and driven them into the troubles and confusions of the Reformation period. The American sects, indeed, were isolated and ignorant, and believed themselves to be the only living recipients of Divine Inspiration. They did not know what had happened in the world before, and they advanced, all ignorantly, to the old disasters and the old mistakes.

Their stories present a sad and repellent picture of misguided enthusiasm driving men and women to the verge, and over the verge of insanity. Were it not that the same causes are still producing the same results, it might be better to leave the whole thing unchronicled. But, after all, the history of human thought and human error is interesting and valuable ; and, though there is little in these sects to admire, there is much from which a moral may be drawn.

21

CHAPTER II

AN ACCOUNT OF THE STATE OF SOCIETY AND RELIGIOUS THOUGHT IN AMERICA AT THE BEGINNING OF THE NINETEENTH CENTURY

EVEN before the American War of Independence proclaimed to the whole world that the new Republic was the home of Liberty and Opportunity, the Colonies in New England had been known to offer an escape from some of the oppressions and tyrannies of Europe. The early settlers who made their way to the new land crossed the Atlantic for a variety of reasons, but one of their most frequent impulses was rebellion against the religious conformity required at home.

The Pilgrim Fathers set off across the ocean because they felt an imperative call to worship God after their own fashion, and longed to live in a land where liberty of conscience was allowed ; and it was in this hope that the early Puritans and Quakers settled in Boston, New York and Philadelphia. And as they spread out over the surrounding country they gave to the new civilisation they were founding the definitely Christian and Protestant atmosphere which it wears to this day.

In spite of their reasons for coming to America, the early settlers were not tolerant themselves, as their successors are now. They brought with them a burning flame of religious excitement, and were as full of the zeal of persecution as the ecclesiastical authorities from which they had escaped. Religious cruelties in the seventeenth and early eighteenth centuries were as natural in the new lands as in the old, and the men and women who had left their homes for Christ's sake expelled heretics from their midst, and even burnt and hanged them with a holy joy, firmly believing that everyone who did not share their convictions would be damned.

Among them, as among their contemporaries in Europe, there were witches and witch hunters, and there were prophets and 'inspired' teachers who saw visions and dreamed dreams. There were even unorthodox, or rather semi-orthodox sects, such as the followers of Anne Hutchinson in Boston in 1634. There were, too, several small communistic religious experiments, such as the 'Labadist Community of Protestant Mystics' established in Maryland in 1680, the 'Community of the Woman in the Wilderness' in Pennsylvania in 1694, and the 'Contented of the God-Loving Soul' who were founded in Germantown in the same year. If these phenomena were to be examined in detail they would no doubt be found to be full of interest, but it is likely that they would differ hardly at all from the similar manifestations which were to be seen in England and Germany at the same time. The traditions which the settlers had brought over, and were still bringing over, were all-powerful, and nothing indigenous to America had as yet made its appearance in the religious world.

Religion, in every form which it has taken in the world, has been built upon a great and complex heap of the ruins of former creeds. Local superstitions, the half-remembered myths and folklore of long centuries, are still twisted into the lives of the peasantry of Europe, and the ritual of Catholicism was superimposed upon a foundation of pure Paganism. In America, however, in the seventeenth century, the only antiquity which influenced the Puritans was that which they brought with them. The Indians and their gods were despised and unknown, and had no effect upon the thoughts of the new white settlers ; and the Africans, who came at a later date, were equally separate and apart. No modifying influences crept into the religion of the white men from the rivers and mountains ; no local deities, no nymphs or satyrs haunted the lonely spaces of the new world. The Puritan settlers were afraid of their own imaginations, and detested and feared the influences of poetry. Stark were their doctrines, and rigid their conceptions of life ; and the only latitude they allowed themselves was the weaving of a complex edifice of theological subtlety upon the foundation of their positive belief.

The great Revivals of Jonathan Edwards, in 1740, began what may be called an American school of doctrine ; and that date marks the real starting-point of our enquiry. The impetus which his preaching and his books gave to all the American churches was marked ; and although there was nothing definitely abnormal about his movement, it displayed all the dangerous revival symptoms.

Groaning, shouting and extreme emotional excitement were common, and Edwards himself was dismissed from his pastorate in 1750 after a dispute on the significant question of whether men and women admitted to church during a Revival, but not truly 'converted', should or should not be allowed to partake of the Lord's Supper.

Edwards died in 1758, and after his death a Revivalist party sprang up which was known as the Edwardean, or New Divinity party, and which made a considerable ferment in the land. They split among themselves, and indulged in great controversies on questions of belief ; and one of their chief subjects of concern was the Calvinist doctrine of Predestination, which some of them came to interpret as implying native sinlessness. All this, though it doubtless contained in many instances the elements of really fanatical movements, was not actually led over the edge of doctrinal disputing into the morass of mystical experiment. It did, however, have the effect of preparing the way for what was to come later, by accustoming men's minds to new teaching, and it planted the beguiling thought of natural sinlessness in a soil where it was destined to flourish.

During the years which preceded the Revolution new interests came to mitigate the bitterness of religious disagreement. Politics ran theology hard for the first place in men's thoughts, and for a time the great ideas of national independence and social equality held the field. The men who fought the War against England, and who adopted the Declaration of Independence and the American Constitution were not concerned to persecute each other for their religious beliefs. Toleration was part of their great doctrine of Liberty ; and they thought they were establishing freedom through the length and breadth of their land.

In truth, however, the liberty and tolerance of the people of the country would not stand very strict examination. Judged by tests such as any school of philosophical thinkers might have applied, the actual individual practice fell very far short of the great ideals embodied in the Declaration of Independence. Wherever enough people were collected together for a village or a township to grow up, the pressure of social convention was overwhelming, and the inhabitants of the young Republic found themselves, and were content to find themselves, enjoying ' life, liberty and the pursuit of happiness ' along almost exactly parallel lines.

The fact that people necessarily lived in small and isolated villages, or in the still more widely scattered outposts of the West, accentuated this tendency. Nowhere is the grip of convention so strong as in small villages ; nowhere is it so essential to think and speak and act exactly like one's neighbours ; and nowhere is the pressure of other people's opinions so overwhelming. The villagers of New England, as they journeyed West founded new settlements on the pattern of those they had come from, they carried with them their ideas, their religion and their social taboos, and planted them as firmly and as successfully as their crops and orchards.

The impulse towards liberty, indeed, seemed to

have been exhausted with the War of Independence. The French Revolution, which set such strong currents of Liberalism flowing in Europe hardly touched the people of America at all. Their own Revolution had contributed directly to the conflagration in Europe, and they thought they had no need of further development. The 'effete monarchy' had been thrown off, and the traces of social inequality wiped away from the laws. All men—all white men at least—were already free and equal in the young United States, so why should they bother with foreign theories, or foreign turmoils? Neither the reaction which swept over Europe in the first years of the new century, nor the Radical revival which succeeded it had any counterpart in America ; and, unknown to themselves, the people of the great new country settled into a rigid social conservatism as oppressive, and as fatal to individual liberty as the 'yoke' they had so triumphantly thrown off.

The uniformity of the ways of life and thought throughout the country was indeed in flat contradiction to the generally accepted idea of what America was like. Theoretically all men were declared free. In sober fact, however, chattel slavery was a settled institution, and remained in force for years after it had been abolished in the rest of the civilized world. Legally and on paper all opinions might be held, and all religions practised ; actually everyone thought very much alike, and variations from the general Puritan assumptions in religion led to social ostracism if not to tarring and feathering in a very short time. Politically the democracy was complete ; yet, until the question of slavery entered the field, there were practically no divisions of principle among politicians, no schools of Radicals, no group of philosophical thinkers, no effective or recognized opposition to things as they were. The system of civilization seemed to be so deeply rooted in the consent of the people that no attention was paid to it ; and the whole force and energy of the time was poured into the task of settling and developing the vast new land.

These facts must be borne steadily in mind in considering the oddities which we are about to chronicle. Numerous and remarkable as these were, and wild as were their claims to universality, they were all of them really insignificant in the history of the United States, and the exaggerated and freakish atmosphere in which they had their rise must not be taken as typical of early nineteenth-century America. It was indeed peculiar to that country and that time. The world has never seen its like before, and probably never will again ; but for all that it is but a bypath, an excrescence upon the normal history of the period, which was in the main a time of steady and sane national expansion, and of the conquest by civilization of the great unpeopled spaces of the West.

The mere fact of the size of the country, taken with the theoretical liberty of which its people were so proud, made these experiments possible. Men, if they were strong enough, and rebellious enough, *could* make their way against the uniform pattern of the time, and attract adherents and followers. And when they did so there was nothing external to stop them short. There was room enough for new experiments, and there was credulity and ignorance enough too, so that America, for all its conformity, offered a field for strange and wild social and religious theories, in which the bold and adventurous could sow what seeds they chose. In the early and middle years of the nineteenth century queer crops grew up from these sowings. The tale of their planting and their ripening is strange ; their harvest, when it came, was sorrow and disillusion ; and it would have been better had the seed fallen by the wayside for the birds of the air to devour.

CHAPTER III

AN ACCOUNT OF THE FOREIGN RELIGIOUS SECTS IN AMERICA IN THE EARLY NINETEENTH CENTURY

THE new world, to which so many religious refugees turned in hope, if it was not all that they imagined, still offered them great and substantial advantages over the homes they fled from. There was plenty of room, and a good living for such as were hard working and thrifty ; there was legal toleration, and freedom from the oppressive interference of State or Church schools, and from military service ; and there was a refreshing absence of respect for authority. All these things were what they were seeking, so that their dreams and hopes were satisfied. America was, to them, the Promised Land.

Apart from the Quakers, the first religious vagaries to find a footing in America came from Germany. In that country the storms and turmoils of the Reformation period had left an active religious ferment which had never entirely died down. Peasant sects underwent spasmodic persecution for their beliefs, and new revivals expressing the old Quietist and Anabaptist doctrines broke out again and again, and refused to be suppressed.

These peasant sects were closely related to movements which had persisted in Christendom from earliest times. Some of their beliefs were held by the Gnostics of the second century, and by the Encratites and the Novatians of the third and fourth. They resembled the Montanists of the second to the sixth centuries, and almost exactly paralleled the Waldenses who suffered persecution in the Alps from the eleventh to the end of the sixteenth centuries. They had a strong likeness to the 'Friends of God', who spread through the Rhine Valley in the year 1300, and they were derived in strict historical descent from Wyclif and the Lollards, and from John Huss of Bohemia, who was burnt at the stake for his beliefs in 1415. The writings of the mystic, Jacob Boehme (born in 1575) were the cause of repeated revivals in Switzerland, Bohemia and South Germany, and these, when diffused among a people already predisposed to receive them by their Anabaptist tendencies, led to the formation of a great many distinct, but similar sects.

There is no need to trace out the details of their genealogies. Their main principles were always much the same ; a belief in the possibility of present-day inspiration, a literal acceptance of the Bible, and an absolute refusal to recognize the authority of either Church or State. Their adherents were gentle, harmless people, stubborn in their opposition to military service and in their determination to teach their children in their own way, and impassioned in their rejection of the Sacraments. Most of them were believers in adult Baptism—in some cases by immersion ; they held ceremonial Agapae, or love feasts, and practised the Oriental custom of washing each other's feet. In all things they followed as closely as they could what they believed to be primitive Christianity, and generally believed with Saint Paul, that marriage was evil. Very few of them were able to exclude it altogether, but, even when they were obliged to recognize it, they held it to be an inferior state to celibacy, and much to be discouraged. Like the early Christians they had a distinct communistic tendency, believing themselves to be only the stewards of the Lord's property, and they were nearly always vegetarians, as well as abstainers from wine and tobacco.

These inoffensive sects were bitterly persecuted in Europe all through the seventeenth and early eighteenth centuries, and at the end of the seventeenth century a group of Mennonites left their native land and set out for America, the country of Promise and Liberty. They called themselves the 'Brethren of the Free Spirit', and were affectionately known as ' The Harmless People ' by their new neighbours ; and they settled down in German-speaking colonies in peace.

The Mennonites had been founded by a Dutchman in 1536, and they were divided into several distinct groups, known by different names, such as the Apostolic, Reformed, Defenceless, etc. The most important of these groups was the Amish, which separated from the parent sect in about 1700, before the emigration to America. These, as well as the parent sect, journeyed to the Promised Land, and came to be known there as the ' Hookers', because they had a scruple about wearing buttons, and fastened their clothes with hooks.

About the year 1725 one of these Mennonite groups was joined by one Conrad Beissel, a German who had come to America hoping to join the 'Woman in the Wilderness Community', which however had ceased to exist. This man was a mystic, who lived for some years as a hermit, and during this period he received the revelation that Saturday was the true Sabbath day. He published this belief, and was joined by five followers, three men and two women, who settled near him in his solitude. Gradually other converts came, and in 1732 a regular communistic society was formed among them, and dwellings (built according to Biblical instructions without nails) were set up, and the place was called EPHRATA. The people lived with the utmost simplicity, most of them remaining celibate, and at first they adopted a peculiar dress. Until Beissel's death in 1786 the community prospered greatly in the only ways it wished to prosper, namely, in harmony and spiritual peace ; but when his influence was withdrawn its membership diminished. It did not break up, however, and in 1900 there were still seventeen persons who professed its faith.

In 1800, fourteen years after Beissel's death, an American preacher named Peter Lehman visited Ephrata, and was so greatly impressed with what he saw there that he determined to found a similar colony in his own town of Snowhill. At first he had only four members, but by 1814 they were forty, and they built a Cloister, a Chapel, a Brother House and a Sister House, and established what was really a monastery without vows which endured for many years, but had ceased to exist by 1900. Both this and the Ephrata Community itself seem to have been quiet and orderly places, with no trace of fanaticism or exaggeration, and so too were the Moravians, or Hussites, who reached America in 1740, and who still form a considerable and distinct group.

Benjamin Franklin, in his Autobiography, gives an interesting account of a Moravian village, and in particular describes their views on marriage in 1756.

' I enquired,' he says, ' concerning the Moravian marriages, whether the report was true that they were by lot. I was told that lots were used only in particular cases ; that generally, when a young man found himself disposed to marry, he informed one of the elders of his class, who consulted the elder ladies that governed the young women. As these elders of the different sexes were well acquainted with the tempers and dispositions of their respective pupils, they could best judge what matches were suitable, and their judgments were generally acquiesced in ; but if, for example, it should happen that two or three young women were found to be equally proper for the young man, the lot was then recurred to. I objected, if the matches are not made by the natural choice of the parties, some of them may chance to be very unhappy. " And so they may," answered my informer, " if you let the parties choose for themselves " ; which, indeed, I could not deny.'

A sect similar to the Moravians came to America from Germany in 1719, and was known as the Dunkers, or Tunkers ; and another, about the same time from Denmark, called the Schwenfeldians ; and both these settled, as the Moravians and Mennonites had settled, in Pennsylvania. In 1804 the number of these German-speaking settlers was increased by the arrival of ship-loads of the followers of George Rapp. These people struggled for some years against great material hardships, and in 1814 they sold out their land in Pennsylvania, and removed to Harmony, Indiana, where they were far more prosperous. The Rappites differed somewhat from the other German sects which had come before, in that they believed that the Second Coming of Christ would occur before the death of their leader, and several other curious things as well. Adam, they thought, had been created in the exact image of God, a dual being both male and female, and if he had been content to remain in his original state he would have produced offspring spontaneously. These beliefs did not make much practical difference in their lives, which were so prosperous and easy that their leader presently became anxious lest their growing leisure should allow time for mischief and rebellion. Accordingly he decided, in 1825, to move the whole settlement away from their village of Harmony, and to begin again in a new place. He sold all the land, with the farms and the village as they stood, to Robert Owen, and, as we shall see, it became under his management the scene of a different communistic experiment. The Rappites, meanwhile, removed to a place in Ohio, which they named ECONOMY, and there they again established themselves in prosperity.

Rapp himself was a very remarkable man, one of those simple good men 'before whom no evil can stand'. He was ready to receive and believe, all who came to see him ; and one of the chief features of his settlement was the unquestioning hospitality with which all travellers, whether honest seekers or mere beggars and rogues, were admitted, housed and fed. This trustfulness, however, very nearly led to disaster when, in 1832, a deliberate impostor entered the community and endeavoured to capture it for himself. This man, whose name was really Bernhard Müller, gave himself out to be a Count Maximilian de Leon, and claimed that he had a special revelation which was written in a Golden Book. According to this revelation the simplicities, the vegetarianism, and particularly the chastity of the Rappites were condemned, and during the winter that he stayed at Economy he turned 250 Rappites from their allegiance. Five hundred, however, remained faithful, and Müller with his followers was obliged to go away ; though they managed to take a large part of the wealth of the community with them. Rapp himself was undismayed by these events. 'The tail of the Serpent', he said, quoting from the Book of Revelation, ' drew the third part of the stars of Heaven and did cast them to the Earth'. And indeed this seemed to be their fate. In a very short time the seceding members had used up the $105,000 they had taken, and came back to ask for more. When it was refused they fell to quarrelling among themselves, and finally set upon and nearly killed Müller, who had claimed that he would make gold for them from stones, but had failed to do so. He was obliged to make his escape, and died soon after, and all his followers dispersed.

The real Rappites, relieved by the withdrawal of all their unstable and discontented elements, entered upon their period of greatest prosperity, and continued to flourish until Rapp's death in 1847. This event was unexpected to the very last. As he lay on his death-bed, and almost with his last breath he reaffirmed his original belief, ' If I did not know that the dear Lord meant I should present you all to Him ', he murmured, ' I should think my last moments had come '. They had ; and with his loss the community began slowly to decline. They lingered a long time, but in 1892, being then but a tiny handful, they wound up their joint affairs and dispersed, and only four of them were living in 1903.

Another party of German peasants was helped by the English Quakers to escape from persecution, and in 1817 they were led from their homes by Joseph Bimeler and reached the shores of the Promised Land. These people called themselves ' Separatists ' and settled at Zoar, and they were more closely allied to the Quakers in their beliefs than any of the other religious emigrants. They made a great point, for example, of not taking oaths, or uncovering the head in greeting or prayer, and they said ' thee and thou ' to all men. They also condemned organized prayer, as being a mere ' babbling with the mouth ' ; but, unlike the Quakers, they were exceedingly fond of music. They had been founded in the first place by a servant girl called Barbara Grubermann, who had been much given to trances in which she claimed to escape to the other world and receive divine revelations. She had died before the emigration to America, and had been succeeded by Bimeler, a man of greater organizing ability, but less prophetic attainments. On their first arrival they were a celibate community, but in 1836 they modified their views, and allowed, but did not encourage, a restricted kind of marriage for the sole purpose of recruiting their numbers with children. And in spite of this they still preserved a community life as far as they could, and discouraged the establishment of separate households. They held that second marriages, even after the death of one party, were absolutely forbidden ; and in this they were of course reopening one of the oldest controversies of the Christian era, and following the rule laid down by Tertullian the Montanist in A.D. 205. As time went on they found that their restricted form of marriage was difficult in practice, and they gradually reverted to 'familism', though still keeping their belief about re-marriage. As the young people born of these first marriages grew up, however, it became impossible to prevent them from coming into contact with, and being contaminated by, the world. Bimeler himself died in 1853, at which time the Community numbered five hundred ; but it steadily decreased. Bicycles completed the emancipation of the younger members, and they rode away, leaving only the old people to carry on the old faith, and in 1898 the Community was, by agreement, brought to an end.

38

The AMANA Society, or the Colony of True Inspiration, was the next to come, in 1842 ; and by 1846 eight hundred people were established at a village which they called EBENEZER, near Buffalo. This group, like the Separatists at Zoar, had had a considerable history before their arrival in America, having taken their rise from the teachings of Eberhard Gruber and Johann Rock in 1714, who in their turn had been influenced by Spener and the ' Inspirationists ' of the last years of the seventeenth century. The sect had congregated at Hesse, where there was more toleration than elsewhere, and in course of time the leadership passed into the hands of Barbara Heinemann, a young woman whom they believed to be the vehicle of present-day inspiration. Barbara, however, fell into disgrace for having ' too friendly an eye to the young men', and when she actually married in 1823 the ' gift ' was thought to have entirely deserted her. Christian Metz became the leader, and it was to him that the revelation concerning emigration was vouchsafed. Under his rule the settlers prospered, and in 1849, when Barbara's husband died, the gift of prophecy was restored to her and she and Metz ruled together. The chief peculiarities of this group, over and above those common to all the German sects, were a shaking when under inspiration, and a public spiritual examination and confession in which all took part. Although a woman was one of their leaders, and unmarried women and widows over thirty were allowed a voice in the temporal affairs of the Community, they still preserved the theory of the early Fathers that there was something peculiarly sinful in the female sex. ' Fly from the society of womenkind as much as possible', one of their precepts ran, 'as a very dangerous magnet and magical fire', a saying almost word for word the same as one of the maxims which Manu laid down for the Hindu world in the year 1000 B.C. Metz died in 1867, and Barbara in 1883, but the Community continued, and in 1908 it still numbered over 1200.

These main groups of foreign religious immigrants were succeeded in the middle years of the nineteenth century by three more. The Bethel and Aurora Communities, which began in 1844 and 1855 respectively were founded by a Doctor Kiel, who claimed to be the First Witness mentioned in the Book of Revelation, and who was joined by small groups of poor and very dirty believers. These communities came to an end in 1880 and 1881. The Bishop Hill Commune, also a very poor group, began in Sweden in 1830 under Eric Janson, and settled in America in 1846. These people believed Janson to be a reincarnation of Christ, and confidently expected that, through him, God was about to build the New Jerusalem, over which he and his heirs were to reign forever. When he was murdered in 1850 in a quarrel which arose between a husband who wished to leave the community and a wife who wished to remain, the whole basis of the belief was shaken, and though they lingered on for another twelve years their unity was completely destroyed.

In 1862 another group of colonists arrived, this time

from Southern Russia, though they were in reality Germans, an offshoot of the Mennonites, who had fled into Russia to escape persecution, only to find it awaiting them there. These people founded three small colonies, called Bruderhof Communities, whose doctrines and discipline were very simple and primitive, and who attached the utmost importance to the details of Church organization. But with their arrival the influx of foreign sects came to an end. Toleration was extending in Germany, and, except for the Dukhobors, who went from Russia to Canada at a much later date, no similar migration seems to have taken place.

All these sects and communities, as we have seen, were simple and primitive. They were not themselves led into fanatical excesses of conduct, and seldom gave rise to them indirectly. Their importance to this history is, however, great. For by their very quietness, and the success which attended their ways of living in the early years, they made the practising of strange beliefs seem possible and safe. Their neighbours grew used to the fact that people could receive special inspiration from On High and yet could remain honest and successful farmers ; and thus the way was smoothed for the more extraordinary and fantastic manifestations which were to spring up.

All these sects were, and continued to be, foreign. They were German speaking from start to finish, and consequently they gained few adherents from among their English-speaking neighbours ; and when, in

41

time, their children and grandchildren began to have dealings with the outside world, the result was not the conversion of the countryside, but the decay of the old foreign faith.

Very different, however, was the influence of the last of these foreign experiments which we must chronicle, namely, the Shakers. These people came originally from England, and were therefore more immediately accessible to their neighbours ; and the effect which they produced upon American religious eccentricities was far reaching.

Ann Lee, the founder of the Millennial Church, or the United Society of Believers, commonly known as Shakers, was born in Manchester in 1736. She was the daughter of a blacksmith, and as a child was employed in a cotton mill, and was not taught to read or write. In her girlhood she came under the influence of a sort of Quaker revival, and with others of the sect she was thrown into prison in 1770 on account of the violent manifestations of her religious fervour. While in prison a new and special revelation came to her, which made clear all the mysteries of the universe, and in particular showed her that God had a dual nature, being both male and female, and that the original sin by which mankind lost the Garden of Eden was the sin of sexual intercourse. On her release from prison Ann Lee began to preach this new doctrine, and as a preparation she separated from her husband, Abraham Stanley, who however still continued to follow her about and became one of her disciples. Very few others accepted her teaching, but in 1771, acting on another special revelation, she set off with eight companions, six men and two women, to found the 'Second Christian Church' in America. Abraham Stanley was one of this small company, but on the way over he seems to have lost his faith, and made love to one of the other passengers on the ship ; and on arrival in America he disappeared from among the group. The others found no immediate way of setting up their new Church, and Mother Ann was content to wait in patience, earning her living as a washerwoman, until the ways of the Lord should be manifest. Four years passed in this way, and then there came a revival among the members of the Baptist church at New Lebanon, a village close to the small settlement over which she presided. These Baptists, being already worked up to a state of religious excitement by their revival, eagerly welcomed the further light and the new doctrine which Mother Ann offered, and thus a beginning was made. Two years passed in missionary effort, during which time Mother Ann went about the surrounding villages preaching, and a wonderful legend grew up. Miracles were constant, and before long it was widely believed that she herself was the second incarnation of Christ. As was natural, such extravagant talk horrified many of the farmers, and they were still more outraged by her insistence upon celibacy. The notion of its holiness, when once it took root in a family, led to constant difficulties and distresses, and persecutions from the unconverted fell upon Mother Ann and her followers. As so often

43

happens, persecution led to more enthusiasm and an increase of membership, and the strength of the Shakers grew. No definite community life was attempted for many years, and it was not until after the death of the foundress, in 1784, that any of the settlements were built. Under the joint leadership of Joseph Meacham and Lucy Wright, both of whom were of American birth, the building of the dwellings and meeting houses began and by 1800 several settlements were in existence.

The Shaker Communities, of which there came to be 27, with a membership of over 5000, were really small villages, made up of dwelling houses for the sisters and for the brothers, meeting houses and barns and sheds for the necessary work of the community. Everything about them was always scrupulously neat and kept in perfect repair, and by their careful husbandry and diligence the Shakers became prosperous and rich. They devoted themselves mainly to growing and preserving fruit, medicinal herbs and garden seeds, and the excellence of their produce was known from one end of the country to the other. The communities were strictly celibate in accordance with the belief about original sin, but they adopted children in large numbers, and educated and trained them in the Shaker faith, hoping to continue their existence. No pressure was put upon these children to remain in the fold if they did not feel a vocation, and, in fact, most of them subsequently left, and went out into the world, and the 'families' were recruited by adult converts year after year. In 1908 there were still fifteen of these settlements in existence, though within a few years most of them came to an end, and only a very few aged members remained.

The manner of life of these Shaker communities was at all times highly esteemed. They were honest and peaceful, kindly, quiet and gentle, and entirely free from scandal of any kind. They were, indeed, settlements of men and women who lived a common life, and worked and prayed together while preaching and practising celibacy ; but all witnesses testify to their entire sincerity and simplicity, and to their transparent honesty. A sweet and gentle spirit seemed to prevail over all the villages, such as is to be found now and then in the convents and religious houses of other creeds ; but the Shaker settlements had a peculiar and unique basis in that their members were bound by no vows, and were free, both legally and actually, to depart at any time.

The good repute of the Shakers, and their worldly success, combined to give some standing to their strange doctrines ; and although most people did not accept their faith, it is evident that it modified and influenced a good many of the surrounding creeds.

The articles of the Shaker doctrine, when looked at apart from the pleasant Shaker atmosphere, were startling enough. They not only believed that God was male and female, but that the second incarnation of Christ had been female, in the person of Mother Ann Lee. The Millennium, they thought, had begun in 1774, and the end of the world was to be brought about by the adoption on all sides of the celibacy they practised themselves. The five most important aspects of the true Church, as they saw it, were, community of goods, celibacy of life, separation from the world, non-resistance, and control over physical disease. They themselves attained the first four of these, and they confidently expected to attain the fifth ; and to these five cardinal points they added, in time, a sixth, namely, the power to hold intercourse with spirits. This development, which did not arise among them till fifty years after their founder's death, preceded by a few years, as we shall see, the popular outburst of spiritualism in the world outside ; but whether it was the cause of this phenomenon, or merely a part of it, it is hard to be sure.

The form of worship which the Shakers practised, and which gave them their popular name, was extremely curious. It consisted in a holy marching and dancing, accompanied sometimes by the singing of Shaker hymns, and sometimes by outbursts of gibberish, believed to be inspired utterances. The brothers and sisters danced in separate groups, moving more or less rhythmically in rows, with their elbows at their sides and their hands held before them ; but when there were seasons of revival, or outbursts of spiritualistic fever, they rolled violently upon the ground, and shook and quivered with the inrush of the spirit. A little preaching, and an occasional confession of sinfulness varied the proceedings, but they had no set or regular prayers, believing that God does not need spoken words, and that their whole lives should be prayer.

The articles of the Shaker faith, though they had a quaintly original form, were of course exceedingly ancient. Long before the Christian era there were settlements of celibate men and women who led communistic lives and adopted children to succeed them. The Shakers, indeed, had much in common with the Essenes of the time of Christ, and still more with the Abstinentes or Spiritales of Spain in the fourth century. Their form of worship by dancing, too, was not original to themselves, and though to the outward view they did nothing at all resembling the practices of the Dancing Dervishes, or the Bacchanalian orgies, the impulse which moved them was doubtless much the same. But neither they, nor any who saw them, gave a thought to such things.

The oddity of their religious exercises, and the report of their queer beliefs attracted innumerable visitors to their doors, and idle sightseers and earnest enquirers alike left Mount Lebanon, or Watervliet, or Pleasant Hill impressed with the saintly happiness and the restful atmosphere of the ' United Society of Believers.'

CHAPTER IV

MILLER, FINNEY, AND THE TRANSCENDENTALISTS

THE first impulse towards abnormal religious movements of native American origin came, as we have seen from the preaching of Jonathan Edwards, and the school of doctrine which arose after his death. The influence of this movement led straight to Revivalism ; and the dangerous and hysterical outbreaks into which Revivalism degenerated in the early years of the century gave rise to nearly all the subsequent religious delusions.

Before we consider Revivals, however, we must notice one small and isolated sect which arose in 1786, and which is interesting from several points of view. In the first place it was led by a woman, a peculiarity which has arisen from time to time all through the Christian era, but which took a firmer hold, and put forth more astonishing fruits in nineteenth-century America than in any other time or place. The woman in question was Jemima Wilkinson, a Quaker girl of twenty years old, who died, and was mourned, and prepared for burial. Just as the funeral was about to leave the house, however, Jemima came to life ; and the miracle naturally led her to believe herself specially chosen of God. She thought that while she had been absent from the body she had been given a special commission to raise up an elect Church which should share with her the joys of the first Resurrection, which event was to arrive before her second death. This doctrine Jemima preached, and many people believed her ; and presently she led a band of followers five hundred miles westward into the wilderness to a place called Crooked Lake, where they established a celibate communistic settlement to await the coming of the Lord.

Jemima was a tall and active woman, so sure of her divine mission that she felt free to dispense with the ordinary conventions of her sex. She wore kilts and a broad-brimmed Quaker hat, such as men wore, and she was absolute ruler over her people. She was a wise and intelligent ruler, and first made friends with the Indian tribes about her, and then so ordered her temporal affairs that the community grew rich. They called her 'The Universal Friend', and when she wanted anything, and said that 'The Lord hath need of it', they gave it to her freely. This settlement prospered from its foundation in 1786 until Jemima's death in 1820 ; but when that unexpected event took place it came to an end. Jemima herself, when she saw death really approaching, had tried to provide against its disruptive effect. She had warned her followers that it might appear as if she were dead, but assured them that 'though she should sleep she would revive again', and had forbidden them to mourn for her, or to give her any ceremonial funeral. They obeyed her as well as they could, and hid her body in a secret place in the ground ;

but they could not wait long for her second revival, and dispersed, sorrowful and disillusioned.

While this community was still in being, the Revival movement broke out in full force, and in 1801 an excellent example of it was seen in the state of Kentucky. Camp meetings were held in the woods, to which people flocked by hundreds, and even thousands, and men, women and small children fell down in convulsions, foaming at the mouth and uttering strange cries under the influence of their excitement. ' They lie as though they were dead for some time without pulse or breath. . . .' wrote an eye-witness. ' To prevent their being trodden underfoot by the multitude they are collected together and laid out in order in two squares of the meeting house, where, like so many dead corpses, they cover a considerable part of the floor. . . . No sex or colour, class or description were exempt from the pervading influence of the Spirit ; even from the age of eight months to sixty years. . . .' Groanings, shoutings and speaking with tongues were constant occurrences, and the preachers would at times creep along the ground, crying out that they were 'the old serpent who had tempted Eve', and exhorting their hearers to ' agonise ' and be saved. Amid all this turmoil the people of the lonely country places found some of the emotional outlet, and even some of the intellectual interest which they lacked in the ordinary course of their lives, and they ' agonised ' and ' repented ' with a will.

The Kentucky Revival has been remembered because the Shakers took advantage of it to recruit new members for themselves, and left a record of the occurrence ; but the practice was not confined to the South, nor to the year 1801. At any time, and in any place, a similar outburst was liable to occur, and being by its very nature highly contagious, it often spread far from its original starting-point. Spasmodic Revivals went on all through the next thirty years, of which the most famous was Nettleton's Revival of 1817 ; but nothing of unusual interest seems to have resulted from them until the time of Miller and Finney, about the year 1831.

William Miller, the founder of a sect which had an immense popularity between 1831 and 1845, was one of those prophets who base their doctrine upon inter-pretations of the Book of Revelation. There are many strange texts in this book, which, if taken literally, and interpreted with sufficient care, can be made to prove that the end of the world is due to arrive at any date which may be desired. Miller selected the date 1843 ; but his calculations have been challenged by innumerable other computations. In the earliest days of Christianity the Second Coming of the Lord was expected before the death of the Apostles, and for several centuries it was almost hourly looked for. St. Augustine killed this belief, but his words, if taken literally, implied that the true date was the year 1000, and about that time the idea revived again, and formed one of the impulses which animated the Crusades. In 1200 the Second Coming was again expected, and in the period just preceding the Reformation the Papacy was widely believed to represent the power of Anti-Christ, which must arise before the Judgment Day. In England alone these predictions were numerous. In 1593 John Napier declared that the end of the world would come before 1688 and when that failed he selected 1700 ; in 1627 Joseph Mede set it for 1660 ; Isaac Newton thought it was imminent in 1733, and in 1734 William Whiston announced it for 1866. Edward Irving thought the true date was 1864, and many others have made equally incorrect estimates. Pastor T. C. Russell, indeed, seemed at one moment to be on the right track. He announced that the Millennium had begun invisibly in 1874, and that the end of the world would follow in 1914 ; but although his adherents were much encouraged by the events of that year, they have since been disappointed.

Outside England the prophets have been equally numerous, and equally mistaken. 1535, the year when John of Leyden occupied Munster as the New Jerusalem and led the inhabitants into the wild orgies and excesses of the Anabaptist outbreak, was perhaps the most famous of these final years, but 1689, 1730 and 1836 were also chosen dates, and each one of these years has been established conclusively by a reference to Holy Writ.

It is a curious fact, in connection with many of these prophecies, that even when the appointed year has passed by, and the end of the world has not come, the believers still hold to their beliefs. A hundred ingenious devices are at once suggested for amending the calculations, and putting the great event off to a slightly later date. Sometimes the calculations themselves still hold good, but the Lord is supposed to be granting a short special dispensation so that the 144,000 who are to be Sealed may be gathered together. One way or another the faithful insist on cheating themselves with the hope that what they have believed for years may still be true, even in the face of the flat contradiction of nature ; and thus no sudden or dramatic end comes to these sects, but Second Adventism lives and survives each one of its disappointments.

The followers of ' Father ' William Miller were no exception to this rule. When the fateful year 1843 passed by, and even the next year followed in safety, they did indeed begin to disagree among themselves, and by 1845 they had split into seven sections, dividing on minor points, such as the correct day for the Sabbath, the necessity for following the Jewish customs in regard to food, and so on. But the power of their main belief did not waver, and to this day adherents of the seven sects earnestly and sincerely expect the sudden and triumphant ending of this world, and the literal coming of all the marvels of the seven angels, the book sealed with the seven seals, the seven last plagues, the beast with the seven heads, and the New Jerusalem with its walls of precious stones, which will descend out of Heaven and stand on the banks of the river of the water of Life.

While the Millerites were dreaming of these things, and growing from month to month in strength and number, Charles Finney's Revival was sweeping through

Massachusetts and Western New York and all the surrounding districts. This Revival was somewhat different from the usual species, in that it left behind it consequences which lasted for a considerable time. It is particularly important in connection with the story of American sects, because it gave the first impetus to the career of John Humphrey Noyes, who, as we shall see later, founded and maintained one of the most extraordinary of the curious religious systems we are examining.

Finney's Revival swept over state after state, sowing strange seeds ; and it lasted for nearly four years. The districts which were affected came to be known as ' the burnt districts,' and the people who lived in them passed their days in a state of constant emotional excitement. In 1834, when this Revival was in full swing, it attacked a young woman named Lucinia Umphreville, who lived in the village of Manlius, and she felt called upon to begin to preach. Her chief concern was the subject of sex, and she believed that everything connected with it was unrelievedly wicked. Under her leadership the young ladies of the neighbourhood began to reject all thoughts of marriage, and instituted in its stead a system which they called 'spiritual marriage'. This state was reached when men and women who were spiritual affinities came in contact with each other, and one of the main signs by which it could be recognised was that holy kisses might be exchanged between them without danger of arousing passionate feelings. This was, indeed, the test of spiritual union, and the young ladies were said to experiment widely before finding their true mates. They maintained, moreover, that people married in the ordinary way were performing a higher duty if they separated and united with their spiritual partners ; and many such separations took place. The spiritual husbands and wives, it was said, carried their tests far beyond the limits of spiritual kissing ; and, so long as they were able to persuade themselves that they did not feel the ordinary human passions, their conduct appeared to themselves highly commendable.

At Brimfield, Massachusetts, the same doctrine arose, and a group of its adherents, led by Mary Lincoln, Flavilla Howard and Maria Brown attempted to increase their spiritual virtue by killing the sense of shame which had been put as a curse upon Adam. To this end they introduced the practice of 'bundling', which consisted in entering the bedroom of a young preacher in the middle of the night, and putting themselves into thoroughly compromising situations. So long as they felt that they were acting solely from the love of God they believed that they were sanctified in these performances and the greater the scandal and opprobrium the better they were satisfied that they were making an acceptable sacrifice to the Lord. On one occasion these young women also ran naked through the countryside ; but the commotion caused by this exploit proved too much even for the Revival atmosphere, and their activities were brought to an end.

W. Hepworth Dixon, in his book, 'Spiritual Wives',

gives a detailed account of these occurrences, which were described to him by eye-witnesses. He gives also an interesting letter he received about them from John Humphrey Noyes, the head of the Oneida Community, whose own brand of peculiarity we shall consider in a later chapter. Noyes was a student of religious aberration, as well as a practitioner, and his book, ' The History of American Socialisms ' is a most interesting production. His views on the developments of Finney's Revival are quaint and amusing.

' One dominant peculiarity of the Shakers,' he writes, ' as also of the Bundling Perfectionists, which determined their style of Socialism, was, in my opinion, the LEADERSHIP OF WOMEN. Man of himself would never have invented Shakerism, and it would have been very difficult to have made him a medium of inspiration for the development of such a system. It is not in his line. But it is exactly adapted to the proclivities of women in a state of independence or ascendancy over man. Love between the sexes has two stages, the courting stage and the wedded stage. Women are fond of the first stage. Men are fond of the second. Women like to talk about love ; but men want love itself. Among the Perfectionists the women led the way in the bundling with purposes as chaste as those of the Shakers. For a time they had their way ; but in time the men had their way.

' The course of things may be restated thus : Revivals lead to religious love ; religious love excites passions ; the converts, finding themselves in theocratic liberty, begin to look about for their mates and their paradise.

Here begins divergence. If women have the lead, the feminine idea that ordinary wedded love is carnal and unholy rises and becomes a ruling principle. Mating on the spiritual plan, with all the heights and depths of sentimental love, becomes the order of the day. Then, if a prudent Mother ANN is at the head of affairs, the sexes are fenced off from each other, and carry on their Platonic intercourse through the grating. But, if a wild Mary Lincoln or Lucinia Umphreville is in the ascendant, the presumptuous experiment of bundling is tried ; and the end is ruin. On the other hand, if the leaders are men, the theocratic impulse takes the opposite direction, and polygamy in some form is the result. Thus Mormonism is the masculine form of the more morbid products of Revivals.'

This view, ingenious as it is, is historically false. The practices and self-justifications of the Bundlers were an exact reproduction of those of the ' Brethren and Sisters of the Free Spirit,' who flourished in Germany in the middle of the thirteenth century, and owed none of their inspiration to women. Almaric, their founder, taught that the sins of the flesh were not sins, if done through the love of God, and other sects at other times have had the same idea. The ' Muckers ' of Konigsberg (1823–1836), and the followers of Henry Prince at his Agapemone in Somerset in 1849 had very similar ideas ; but in none of these sects was the leadership in the hands of women. It is interesting to notice, however, that there have been some women teachers who have put forward this idea, the most prominent of whom was Marguerite de Hain-ault, who was put to death by the Inquisition in 1310 for maintaining in theory and practice that the soul absorbed in Divine Love could yield without sin or remorse to the desires and impulses of the body.

The whole history of religious mania, in fact, shows clearly that sex is one of the commonest and most powerful of the influences leading to aberration in the religious world, just as it seems also to be the centre of madness and distortion in ordinary mundane affairs. It is important to remember that there have always been two diametrically opposed ways in which this influence can be made manifest, denial and excess ; and the one is almost as likely to lead to trouble as the other. Of course it would be absurd to maintain that all celibate religious houses are centres of mania, or that there have not been, and are not still, men and women of well-balanced and holy lives who have voluntarily put aside the ordinary sex life of mankind, and have vowed to devote themselves to God. While this is so, however, it would be almost equally absurd to ignore the fact that the glorification of celibacy, which was rife in the early centuries of Christianity, led to many flagrant abuses, and that religious aberrations as well as open scandals, sprang from this cause. The visions and trances and dreams of the saints were matched by visions and trances and dreams of a grosser quality ; and when these were mistaken for Divine guidings, and were followed and imitated on any considerable scale, fanatical outbursts were the inevitable result.

Nearly always the starting-point for the perversion of religious impulses lies in a mystical approach to the Deity. Nothing is so difficult to understand, or at any rate to put into words, as the mystical outlook ; and though much has been written by those who have themselves enjoyed mystical experiences, very little of what they say is really intelligible to those who have not had sensations of their own of the same nature.

Some things about it are, however, fairly clear, and the aspect of mysticism which seems to have had the most direct influence upon the uprising of fanatical sects has been the tendency to regard the existing world of nature as irrelevant, if not actually antagonistic to God. This theory is very ancient, and had probably given rise to strange and terrible practices long before the Christian era ; but in the early centuries after Christ it came to be associated with the Dualistic theory of the universe which entered into so many of the early heresies. The theory that there is active opposition between God and the world leads inevitably to the notion that the human soul and the human body are also enemies ; and asceticism is the inevitable result.

No doubt there are other additional reasons for the prevalence of asceticism in the early Christian Church. It may have been partly a result of Buddhist influences, and partly a survival from savage times. Among the primitive peoples it may have originated as a sort of training for the hardships of life, or as a way of actually mitigating them ; or it may have had some symbolical meaning. We cannot be certain how it originated in the dark ages of the world, but it is evident that it existed, and that it was rationalized and brought into relation with religious theory in the early days of Christianity, and became a widespread and highly esteemed sign of religious devotion. The hermits who retired into the Libyan deserts and all the innumerable followers who have imitated their self-devotion believed that it was only by the destruction, or at least by the subjection of the body and all its natural impulses that the soul could be set free for its true flight towards God ; and that it was only when a man was freed from the trammels of the flesh that true mystic communion could be secured.

At first sight the ascetic ideal would seem to be far removed from the orgies and indulgences which have marked so many fanatical sects, but the connection is in reality close. The object of denying the flesh and torturing and subduing the body was to reach the state of spiritual freedom in which mystical experiences could be obtained, and to enable the individual soul to abandon itself, without thought of this world, to the purest communion with God. This was the ideal ; and it was undeniably the practice of a great many of the saintly figures of all ages. By this road, hard as it is, many human beings have found the satisfaction of their longings, and have felt themselves lifted up into planes of existence where they have met with joys and rewards which other mortals do not understand. There is, however, a parallel path of self-abandonment, much easier to enter and much pleasanter to pursue which, at any rate at the outset, seems to lead to the same results, and that is physical excess. Dreams, visions, trances, and all the outward signs of mystic rapture can be induced by very carnal means, by wine and by music, by drugs and frantic dancing, by hysteria, hypnotism and sexual excess. And along this path many seekers have turned their steps.

The Shakers, indeed, avoided these pitfalls, and walked quietly and happily in their chosen paths ; but the ' Bundlers ' and the Perfectionists, and still more the ' Brotherhood of the New Life,' whom we shall presently consider, lost their way completely and fell into the old snares.

During the period when the Revivals of Miller and Finney were in progress, one of the most famous of all the American sects was coming into being. Joseph Smith, the founder of Mormonism, was born in 1805, and murdered in 1844, and it was in the year 1823 or '24 that he first saw visions of angels, and discovered the golden plates which led him to dictate the Book of Mormon. No description of this sect need be given here. Not only is it well known, and adequately chronicled elsewhere, but it is still a living belief. Its system of polygamy has been abandoned, and many of the strange marvels which marked its origin have grown dim ; but it is still to-day the same Church of the Latter Day Saints as arose in the early nineteenth century, and therefore excluded from discussion here.

One other development of the period must be recorded, however, before we pass to the marvellous year 1843, and that is the Transcendental Movement. This was not strictly a Christian sect, but it was so religious in tone, and so intensely altruistic, that it might almost be classed as a religious movement ; and it was so widely known that it had a marked influence upon the thought of the period.

The Transcendentalists were a New England group, and originated in the ardent discussions of a set of young men and women concerning the everlasting problems of 'the good, the true, and the beautiful'. In 1830 there was in Boston a sort of intellectual aristocracy, and there was a younger generation growing up whose parents and even whose grandparents had lived there before them, and had built up an educated and thoughtful society such as existed nowhere else in the country. It included scholars, and preachers who were known all over the country, and writers whose fame reached across the Atlantic ; and the people who lived there took a solid and enduring pride in the reputation for culture which their state enjoyed. Moreover there were a number of brilliant people in the generation which was growing up there in the first three decades of the century. There were the Channings, Thoreau, Emerson, Hawthorne and Margaret Fuller, for example ; and these young people, intimately acquainted and often related to each other, found it the easiest thing in the world to meet and meet again to discuss the problems of the universe. Many of them were Unitarians, and their background was strictly Puritan, and their ideals magnificently high. They 'hitched their wagons' to stars so far removed from earth that they floated off into dim and attenuated regions of thought, and they sowed their wild oats at Brook Farm.

This famous experiment in community life was first opened in 1841, when George Ripley resigned from the ministry in order to try and 'establish the external relations of life on a basis of wisdom and purity . . . to substitute a system of brotherly co-operation for one of selfish competition . . . and to impart a greater freedom, simplicity, truthfulness, refinement, and moral dignity to our mode of life.' About seventy people joined the community, which depended for its maintenance upon the agricultural work of its members ; but, unlike many similar experiments which followed, the main interest of the members remained intellectual. As one of their admirers put it, they 'had the extraordinary skill to cover their poverty with the attractive veil of poetry, and to infuse charm and romance into their prosaic, everyday occupations. . . . Music, excursions, and literary and scientific discussions filled out all leisure hours.'

No attempt was made to alter the family basis of life, and as there was no 'unitary building' the members lived in several farm houses, more or less scattered and separate. There were a good many children among them, and a special point was made of their school, which endeavoured to teach 'a wide range of sciences and arts, under the skilful and loving guidance of competent instructors'. All this, although so ideal and altruistic was too worldly for some of the Transcendentalists, and in 1843 A. Bronson Alcott, with a few like-minded people, endeavoured to found a really ideal community, where ' mine and thine ' should have no meaning at all. ' The greater part of man's duty ', they believed, ' consists in leaving alone much that he is in the habit of doing ' ; and accordingly they proceeded to omit almost all the normal activities of life. They refused to recognize the existence of money, and tried to substitute barter and exchange ; they not only adopted vegetarianism, but also rejected butter, cheese, eggs, milk, tea, coffee, rice and molasses, and would not burn oil or tallow candles. One man would eat no root which pushed downwards instead of aspiring to the sun, and none of them would consent to wear woollen clothing or leather shoes. They thought that it was wicked to make animals work, either in drawing carts or ploughing the fields, and believed manure to be a ' debauchery of both the earthly soil and the human body'. They rose very early in the morning and began the day with a cold bath and a long music lesson, after which came a breakfast of unbolted wheat cakes and water, followed by work in the fields ; but as they thought weeds had as much right to grow as crops and vegetables their farm was not very successful. The settlement was called Fruit-lands, and it was their idea to make of it a vast orchard (though there was some talk of letting the forests creep over the ploughed lands, and living only on wild berries) ; but the experiment only lasted from spring to winter. When the cold weather came on, and the long evenings set in with only the light of pine knots to disperse the darkness, the members abandoned their ideals and returned to their Boston lives.

This experiment, which was almost a parody of Brook Farm, had only twelve adherents. It is worth mention, however, because it shows up very clearly the general tendency of the Transcendental idealism, and the thin unsubstantial texture of their dreams. They offered nothing solid upon which a new state of society might be based ; yet it was a new state of society for which they were all longing. It is not surprising, therefore, that when the wave of Fourierite Socialism struck the country, the Brook Farmers, as well as hundreds of other people were caught up in its wash. It offered a ready-made and complete solution of all their problems, and seemed for the moment as if it would make the world anew.

CHAPTER V

THE OWEN AND FOURIER MOVEMENTS, AND THE GREAT YEAR, 1843

BEFORE we consider the Fourierite excitement, and all the developments to which it gave rise, we must give some account of the earlier Socialist movement which Robert Owen had introduced into America in 1824. After the success of his experiment at New Lanark Owen had still further enlarged his views of the perfectability of human society, and he went to America in 1824 in the belief that a grand new system of co-operation and community of goods might be instituted. throughout the land. His first plan was to start an experimental colony, and for this purpose he purchased, lock, stock and barrel, the village of Harmony, Indiana, which the Rappites had just left to move to their new home at Economy.

The place was admirably adapted for community life, having three thousand acres of good cultivated land, fine orchards and vineyards, and plenty of housing accommodation, so that the settlers whom Owen collected there began their experiment in 1825 with high hopes. Eight hundred people, whom Owen believed to represent 'the industrious and well disposed of all nations' joined him within the first six weeks. No tests whatever were imposed upon would-be members ; all religions were welcomed, and perfect freedom of discussion on theological and social questions was allowed. Among the members of the settlement there were many sincere and earnest men and women who came to New Harmony because they hoped to further Owen's views and to assist in the foundation of a new world ; but there were also many idlers and adventurers who came for what they could get ; and by this element the privilege of free discussion was wildly abused. They so infinitely preferred talking to working that they kept a continual flow of controversy alive, and summoned general meetings without number to discuss the affairs of the place. Seven different constitutions were adopted in two years, and each one was the occasion of reviving, and re-deciding all the fundamental principles of social philosophy. The free debating of religious matters which was one of the special features of all the schemes led to constant trouble, and added to the stream of talk ; and whisky, too, played havoc among the idlers. It was soon clear, even to the most enthusiastic, that the atmosphere which prevailed at New Harmony was very inharmonious indeed, and Owen himself was almost the only one who remained hopeful. On the 4th of July, 1826, he made what he called ' The Declaration of Mental Independence ', and inveighed in a grand oration against ' the awful Trinity of man's oppressors,—the most monstrous evils that could be combined to inflict mental and physical evil on the whole race—Private or Individual Property,

Absurd and Irrational Systems of Religion, and Marriage founded on Private Property combined with some of these Irrational Systems of Religion'. Their alternative at New Harmony, he declared, would 'spread from Community to Community, from State to State, from Continent to Continent, until this system and this TRUTH shall overshadow the whole earth, shedding fragrance and abundance, intelligence and happiness upon all the sons of men'.

Alas for these hopes ! Within a very few months two bands of his own people had broken off and settled for themselves at ' Macluria ' and ' Feiba Peven,' [1] and within a year the whole place had reverted to the system of individualism, and the experiment was at an end.

' I wanted honesty of purpose,' said Owen, ' and I got dishonesty ; I wanted temperance, and was continually troubled with the intemperate ; I wanted industry, and I found idleness ; I wanted cleanliness, and I found dirt ; I wanted carefulness, and I found waste ; I wanted to find the desire for knowledge, and I found apathy.' With such material nothing was to be done.

Owen himself was not long discouraged by the failure of New Harmony. He continued to be an optimist and an idealist, and to devise fresh schemes for

---

[1] This curious name was supposed to represent the latitude and longitude of the settlement. According to the notation adopted, *a* and *b* equalled 1, *c* and *d* equalled 2, *ei* equalled 8, etc. Thus *Feiba Peven* stood for 38.11N and 87.53W. On the same principle London becomes *Idfa Tovuten*, and Paris *Olio Ornate*.

the reshaping of the world, and at the end of his life he still justified the description of him given by one of his American friends. ' In years ', said Mr. Adin Ballou (himself the leader of the Community at Hopedale), ' nearly seventy-five ; in knowledge and experience superabundant ; in benevolence transcendental ; in honesty without disguise ; in philanthropy unlimited ; in religion a sceptic ; in metaphysics a Necessesarian Circumstantialist ; in morals a universal excursionist ; in general conduct a philosophical non-resistant ; in socialism a Communist ; in hope a terrestrial elysianist ; in practical business a methodist ; in deportment an unequivocal gentleman.' But for all that he was aware that he had not yet succeeded in ' shedding fragrance and abundance, intelligence and happiness upon all the sons of men '.

The system which Owen advocated was attempted in other places than New Harmony, but with no greater success. Communities were set up at Yellow Springs, Blue Spring, Forrestville, Franklin, Coxackie, Kendal and Haverstraw, but none of them survived for more than one year, and all ended in discord. The ' awful Trinity of man's oppressors ' was too strong for them, and amid quarrels and confusions they melted away.

There was one other offshoot of the Owenite Movement which deserves mention, and that was the settlement at Nashoba, Tennessee. This experiment was intended to combine several theories, and to show the way to a practical solution of the difficult problem of negro slavery. Frances Wright who was its founder was a very interesting woman, who built up for herself a terrible reputation by being in advance of her times, and speaking and writing freely about her revolutionary theories. She was English by birth, and had travelled widely all over Europe, making friends with General Lafayette and all the leading Republicans in France and Italy ; and like so many others she turned to America for the realization of her ideals. She had a great influence over Robert Dale, the most famous of the sons of Robert Owen, and joined him in editing a propaganda paper and in lecturing. At the time of the experiment at Nashoba this missionary effort of theirs had not begun, for they hoped to be able to recommend their ideas by the more valuable and convincing method of practical success ; and Robert Dale Owen was engaged in teaching the school at New Harmony while Frances Wright was busy in Tennessee.

Before founding her colony Frances Wright made some enquiries in the South, and also visited the Rappites at Economy where she watched them build their new village. She also stayed with the Shakers, whom she neither liked nor approved of, and then in 1825, while New Harmony was starting in Indiana, she bought land near Memphis, and launched her plan. The leading idea was to educate negroes so that they might be ready for freedom, and to have black and white families living together in a state of social equality. She bought two or three negro families, and persuaded some rich planters to give her others, and with these people, and a nucleus of white companions, she began the great scheme. Everyone in the community was expected to work, the negroes ' filling occupations which their habits render easy, and which to their guides and assistants might be difficult or unpleasing ', that is to say the work on the plantations and the menial work of the households, and for the whites there were gardening, school teaching, nursing and 'useful trades'. All were to share in the profits of the concern, half the share of the negroes being set aside for the purchase of their freedom. The children were all to be educated together and the results were to be so convincing that the system would presently be adopted wholesale and the troubles of the South brought to an end.

All went well for a time, under the management of Frances Wright herself ; but before long she fell ill, and went away to Europe to regain her health ; and in her absence troubles arose. The Communistic side of the enterprise broke down utterly. As the Trustees she had appointed to manage it truly said, ' thoughts of evil and unkindness, feelings of intolerance and words of dissension which produce in the world only commonplace jealousies and everyday squabbles are sufficient to destroy a Community ' ; and in this case, as in so many others, they did so. Frances Wright made an effort to pull it together on her return, but too much had been lost, and in June, 1828, it broke up. Unlike many Communities, however, though it broke up in dissension, all was not utterly wasted. Frances Wright felt herself responsible for the negro families she had meant to educate, and in the following year she sent them all to Hayti, and established them in freedom there.

The mixture of Communism and Abolition which this experiment embodied was typical of a great deal of the reforming thought of the time. Without exception the adherents of the new causes and the new religions were opponents of slavery, and the regular Abolition Movement was closely intertwined with the other 'Movements' of the day. One of the peculiarities of the extreme Abolitionists was that they really believed in free speech ; and the consequence of this was that their meetings, and still more their Conventions, were overrun by cranks of every description who found a platform for the enunciation of all their fancies. William Lloyd Garrison and the other leaders of the extreme sections of the Anti-Slavery Societies held strong non-resistance principles, and carried their hatred of 'formality' so far that they allowed their business meetings to be directed as the spirit might lead ; and in those days the spirit led in strange directions. People arose among them to preach the sinfulness of shaving, the wickedness of the use of hot water, or the viciousness of taking part in elections. Others sang the praises of Animal Magnetism, Phrenology, Hydropathy, or Universology, and used a queer jargon of long words, 'the Grand Pantarchy,' 'Equitable Commerce,' 'Philo-progenitive Familism,' 'Associationism,' 'The Doctrine of Correspondence with Universal Unity,' and the like. Every one of these 'causes' suffered from the complete democracy of ideas which prevailed ; nothing was too improbable to be considered seriously ; no one was too ignorant to be listened to, while over it all was spread an ever-eloquent ' gift of tongues ', which set all the world disputing. ' Nothingarians ' arose with their cry of, ' No God, No Government, No Marriage, No Money, No Meat, No Tobacco, No Sabbath, No Skirts, No Church, No War, No Slaves, etc.' (which their enemies called, 'No Salt, No Pepper theories'), and threw their scepticism into the hodge-podge of Anti-Slavery, Non-Resistance, Feminism, Spiritualism, Faith Cure, Vegetarianism, Second Adventism, Food Reform, Temperance, Mysticism, Quack Medicines, and Transcendental absurdity.

The whole thing was essentially a revolt from the tight pressure of doctrinal and social conventions in the midst of which the people of America lived. It was a symptom of the intellectual hunger of those who had as yet no literature and no art, a fantastic but pathetic attempt to prove to themselves and to the world that America, freed from the old traditions, could contribute fresh splendours to the world of thought. It is true that the greater number of those who embarked upon this attempt were sadly ill-qualified for the task. Not only were they ignorant of what the world had thought before, and cut off from it by lack of books and of knowledge of languages, history or philosophy, but also they were closely hedged in by the very circumstance of their revolt. It seemed to them more daring, and more important, to challenge the things which were axiomatic among their contemporaries, such as the sinfulness of card-playing and the necessity of observing the Sabbath, than to explore the mysteries of science ; they hardly dared to question the ' authenticity ' of the Bible, and again and again felt that they had ' proved ' a point when they could produce a text to support it. Nevertheless, in spite of the wild and credulous nature of their thought, in spite of its crudity and its absurdity, there was a considerable element which proved to be of value amid all the nonsense. The Anti-Slavery Movement, separated from its extravagant companions, presently shook the whole nation even to the argument of civil war ; and the feminism which took its rise in these wild years lived to triumph in 1918. Temperance led to Prohibition, and non-resistance, though still but a theory, is now finding expression in proposals for world-wide peace pacts, and when the chaff is finally sifted from the grain it may well be that the germs of other great ideas will be discerned in the sayings of the fantastic American prophets of those far-off years.

The ferment of new notions and strange doctrines reached its height in the 'forties. ' We are all a little wild here,' wrote Emerson to Carlyle in 1840, ' with numberless projects of social reform. Not a reading man but has a draft of a new Community in his waistcoat pocket.' He was perfectly right. Projects grew on every bush, and newspapers devoted to reform causes sprang up like mushrooms. These ' organs ' of opinion poured forth floods of eloquence, and did their full duty in exalting both the reforms and the reformers.

'The trump of Reform', wrote the 'Dial' in 1841, 'is sounding throughout the world for a revolution of all human affairs. The issue we cannot doubt ; yet the crises are not without alarm. Already is the axe laid at the root of that spreading tree, whose trunk is idolatry, whose branches are covetousness, war and slavery, whose blossom is concupiscence, whose fruit is hate. Planted by Beelzebub, it shall be rooted up. Reformers are metallic ; they are the sharpest steel ; they pierce whatsoever of evil or abuse they touch. Their souls are attempered in the fires of heaven ; they are mailed in the might of principles, and God backs their purpose. They uproot institutions, erase traditions, revise usages, and renovate all things. They are the noblest of facts. Extant in time, they work for eternity ; dwelling with men, they are with God.'

Phrases such as these sounded almost normal in the 'metallic' ears to which they were addressed, and similar sentiments were eloquently expressed on convention platforms. In 1843 no less than a hundred National Conventions were called together by the Massachusetts Anti-Slavery Society alone, and their organizer, John A. Collins, so arranged matters that a Socialist Convention followed immediately after, at the same town. The consequence of this was that a perfect orgy of political, social and theoretical discussion was carried into almost every State.

1843 was the year in which Albert Brisbane and Horace Greeley let loose their version of Fourierism upon the country ; and it was the year when the world did not come to an end, as the Millerites had expected. It was thus a year prepared for strange happenings ; and it saw them rise.

Albert Brisbane, the American prophet of Fourierism, was a man of considerable education, who had spent much of his life in travel in different parts of the world. He was of the enthusiastic temperament of which reformers are made, and was an ardent disciple of St. Simon until turned aside by the quarrels between Enfantin and Bazard. In 1832, just after the trial of Enfantin, he fell in with Fourier's ' Treatise on Domestic and Agricultural Association', and was at once enthralled. Here was a system which dignified the manual labour of mankind ; here was the true basis of society ! He rushed to Paris, and spent two years sitting at the feet of the Master, absorbing his ideas.

Fourier's ideas were a most curious mixture of sense and nonsense. It is possible to extract from them a scheme of world organisation, as Brisbane did, which, though impracticable, is at any rate theoretically possible, and perfectly coherent. It is also possible to draw from among them a rigmarole of the wildest absurdity ; a statement that the stars and planets eat, drink and make love ; a prediction that the sea will turn to lemonade, and that a new race of animals, called ' anti-horses,' ' anti-lions ' and the like will appear on the earth, and that the ' Couronne Boréal ' will revolutionise the aspect of the globe and cause the world to become one huge Paradise. These parts of the doctrine, as well as the free love element, and the entrancing suggestion of the 'emancipation of the flesh' the disciple seems to have left on one side. He returned to America with the other ideas, however, and published his 'Social Destiny of Man' in 1840, and then began to carry on a vigorous propaganda on behalf of the Principle of Association, as set forth by his Master. In this task Brisbane was immensely helped by Horace Greeley, at that time editing a New York daily paper, the 'Tribune'; and before long a great many serious and substantial men were converted to their Utopian views.

By 1843 this movement had advanced so far that practical experiments were begun, and in that year the first swarm of Fourierite Phalanxes made their appearance. Brook Farm, too, was converted to the faith, and the adhesion of so many well-known and intelligent people gave renewed impulse to the cause.

The basis of the Phalanxes was not unlike that of New Harmony, though there were some differences of detail and organization. All of them aimed at a return to nature, at prosperity through agricultural labour, and at community of goods and interests, estimated by a somewhat complicated method. There was no attempt to secure religious unity, and a description of the course of events at the Clarkson Phalanx, given by one John Greig, an eye-witness, will make clear their practice in this respect. 'As for religion,' he said, 'we had seventy-four praying Christians, including all sects in America, excepting Millerites and Mormons. We had one Catholic family, one Presbyterian clergyman and one

Universalist. One of our Trustees was a Quaker. We had one Atheist, several Deists, and in short a general assortment ; but of Nothingarians, none ; for being free for the first time in our lives, we spoke out one and all, and found that everybody did believe something. All the gospels were preached in harmony and good fellowship. We early got up a Committee on preaching the Gospel, placing one of each denomination upon said Committee, including a Deist, who, being a liberal soul, and no bigot in his infidelity, was chosen Chairman on the Gospel. . . . One word about our Atheist—our poor unfortunate Atheist ; he was beloved by every soul on the domain, and was an intimate friend of our orthodox minister. We had no difficulties on the score of religion.'

If they had no religious troubles at Clarkson (as was not the case at other Phalanxes), they had plenty of material ones. According to the ideal Fourierite plan the Communities should have consisted of four hundred members, each contributing $1000, and there should have been large and comfortable Palaces, in which the members should live together as one large family, raising their own produce, and economizing labour and expense by uniting. The actual arrangements of the Phalanxes were, however, far from this ideal. The groups of enthusiasts who composed them were too impatient to wait until they had collected so many people and so much money, and as soon as they had the barest necessities they rushed forth to the fray. Usually they bought their property on mortgage ; and, being idealists, and city people, they chose barren and unprofitable land, far away from transport facilities or help. On their stony wildernesses they put up a few log cabins, and in these, instead of in the great Unitary Palaces, they huddled together. They found the work hard and trying, and in their ignorance they mismanaged everything, and made no profit at all ; so that by the time the first payments on their mortgages became due they were usually ready to quit.

Of these sad experiments nineteen, besides Brook Farm, were in existence in 1843, and though they varied a little from each other, and were not all strictly orthodox in the Fourierism, they can be classed together as belonging to this main family. They were : the Alphadelphia Phalanx, the Bloomfield Association, the Bureau County Phalanx, the Goose Pond Community (surely an appropriate name), Hopedale, the Jefferson County Industrial Association, the Lagrange Phalanx, McKean County Association, the Marlborough Association, the Moorhouse Union, the Northampton Association, the North American Phalanx, the One Mentian Community (this name signifying that the members were all of one mind), the Ontario Union, Roxbury, the Sylvania Association, the Skeneateles Community, and the Washentaw Phalanx.

A great many of these settlements broke up in the first year, but some were apparently stable. Hopedale, for example, still had 175 members after ten years, but, as its historian relates, ' as the tinsel of novelty wore off other hard actualities of our uncomfortable domestic situation began to overtax our nerves, we lost a portion of our spiritual enthusiasm, firmness and patience. Moreover love, the great disturber of community life, came their way. ' Notwithstanding our vigilance ' he reports, ' there arose in our midst during the year 1853 a case of marital infidelity and illicit intercourse that caused great unpleasantness, perplexity and scandal, and that required at length Community intervention. The story is simply this : One of our male members, the head of a family, became enamoured of a woman, also a member, who had for some time resided in his household, and proportionally estranged from his faithful and worthy wife. Suspicion of something wrong arose among outsiders, causing considerable talk of a scurrilous nature, though nothing was absolutely known. At length the unhappiness of the wife was revealed, and the cause of it, upon investigation, made public. The matter then very properly received attention from the Council, who summoned the delinquents before them for examination and discipline. Upon being questioned and confronted with proof of misconduct, they acknowledged culpability, professed regret and penitence, and promised amendment. But these professions proved insincere, or at least transient, and the parties were again called to account. They then did not deny or attempt to conceal their criminality, but rather justified it on the ground that it was consonant with the principles of the new philosophy concerning personal liberty, sexual relations and the conjugal bond which they had embraced—in a word, they openly and unhesitatingly avowed themselves to be Free Lovers, from conviction and in practice also. Having taken that position they could not do otherwise than withdraw from the Community membership and leave the locality where both their theory and their action were held in almost universal derision and abhorrence.'

This affair did not disrupt Hopedale, but it disturbed the members ; and in the same year an even more unsettling—though decidedly more original—difficulty arose. It was the custom of the Community to allow each member fifty cents a day, and over and above this to pay by the hour for useful work done for the common good. One of the members, Brother Lamson by name, made the suggestion that nursing mothers should be paid as least as much as was paid for any other work, and, his wife having a baby just at that time, he further announced that their job involved, at the mildest, a sixteen-hour day. Payment on this scale would have given the mothers just twice the money earned by skilled workmen, and the principles of the Community could not expand to admit this idea. Fifty cents a day was all they were granted, and Brother Lamson and his family retired. After this difficulties and disagreements multiplied, and Hopedale, like the others, ended in confusion.

The end had not been evident in 1844, and in that year thirteen similar communities had been started, namely : Brooke's Experiment, Ceresco, or the Wisconsin Phalanx, Claremont, the Clarkson Industrial Association, the Grand Prairie Community, the Iowa Pioneer Phalanx,

Leraysville, Mixville, the Ontario and Ohio Phalanxes, Prairie Home, Sodus Bay, and the Trumbull Phalanx. In the following year only three were opened : the Columbian Phalanx, the Integral Phalanx, and the Sangamon Phalanx ; and after that only a few scattered, forlorn hopes ; the Spring Farm Association (1846), Garden Grove (1848), and the Raritan Bay Union of 1853.

Each one of these experiments, which are now but queer-sounding names, stands for a failure, for shattered hopes and wasted money, and for the disillusionment of eager idealists. ' The four great evils with which the world is afflicted ', the Wisconsin Phalanx announced in 1845, ' intoxication, lawsuits, quarrelling and profane swearing, never have and never can find admittance into our society'. But alas ! these evils were too strong. Some of the societies prospered a little more than others, and some lasted a few years ; but all alike ended in disappointment, and, amid their ruins, the Fourierite Movement melted away.

CHAPTER VI

THE SWEDENBORGIAN SPIRITUALISTS

AFTER the failure of the Fourierite Movement, the rage for Utopias somewhat died down. After 1846 there were, indeed, a number of small non-religious experiments, many of them carried on by undiscouraged enthusiasts who had been through the Owen or Fourier mills ; but they none of them attracted any wide following. The first was the Altruist Community on the Mississippi, which was made up of the remains of the North American Phalanx, but had no surer hold on life. Then came Josiah Warren, one of the original members of New Harmony, who, in 1851 struck out a line of his own. He learnt a lesson from the failure of the communistic idea, and flew to the opposite extreme and became a rampant individualist. His first experiment was a ' Time Store ' where he sold goods in exchange for a mixture of money and 'labour notes'. The idea was that he should take the actual money cost of the goods, plus a small percentage for cost of storage, and that his own time should be given in exchange for the time spent by others upon useful work. The labour notes were for periods of from five minutes to an hour, and they were marked with the value the worker put upon his own labour—a matter which caused a good deal of dispute. The women who dealt at the store put a value upon their house work as high as the men put upon their own, and Mr. Warren did not complain of that ; but there were some who debased their own currency by issuing to themselves too many notes, and the system was difficult to adjust. After two years of this complicated book-keeping Mr. Warren founded a small settlement called, without disguise, 'Utopia', and there he tried with three or four families to carry out a plan of Equitable Commerce. This not succeeding according to his hopes, he started again in 1851 at a place called Modern Times, on Long Island, where the plan of bartering services against commodities without the use of money was still further elaborated, and was combined with the fullest freedom to experiment in dress and marriage. But even Modern Times grew out of date, and nothing came of the movement.

In 1851 two small Colonies were founded called Bethel and Berlin Heights, the second largely made up of the remnants of the first. Little is known of them beyond the common countryside rumour that they were free-love colonies, and they seem to have left no record of their peculiarities or beliefs.

No wholesale migration of foreign religious sects seems to have come to the Promised Land after the early years of the century, but several secular, and one or two religious prophets turned their footsteps thither. In 1850, for example, a considerable movement arose at Nauvoo, the town from which the Mormons had just started on their great trek to Utah. This movement called itself 'rationalistic democratic', and was entirely composed of French people. Its leader, Etienne Cabet, came to America in 1848 and tried to found a small colony at Red River, Texas, but owing to yellow fever and other external difficulties it did not flourish. In 1850 or '51, however, he succeeded in making a better start at Nauvoo with 1500 people, among whom community of goods and compulsory marriage were the rule. This colony seems to have quarrelled as much as, if not more than any of the others, and in 1856 poor Cabet was himself expelled, and died with a broken heart a few weeks later. Offshoots of the movement were set up at Icaria in Iowa, and later in California ; but none of them were harmonious, and all were wound up before 1895.

Cedar Vale Community in Kansas began and ended its life in 1871. It was composed of Russians, who called themselves 'Progressive', and allowed their members to believe what they pleased, except that a ' hygienic doctor ' and a ' reformed clergyman ' were provided. Three years later an American ' Social Freedom Community ' arose at Chesterfield, Va, intended to prove the importance of ' Having no religion and no bye-laws, and rejecting the idea of man's total depravity'. It did not succeed in vindicating these ideas any better than the communities which were overwhelmed with constitutions. In 1877 there came to America a pleasanter colony, a group of the young Polish intelligentsia, who believed that they could live almost without working upon the richness of Californian land. They settled at Anaheim, and for one happy year, until their money was gone, they made music, acted plays, discussed philosophy, smoked cigarettes and ate Californian peaches. Then they went home again, disappointed, but not particularly disillusioned, to their native land.

Other colonies with curious names and ancient ideas arose at other dates. There were Tobolampo in Mexico (1886–1891), and the Ruskin Commonwealths in Tennessee (1894–1899), and many more. But those of the end of the century are too recent, and too far removed from the phenomena we are considering to be relevant to our story.

Religious attempts to reform the ways of the world went on at the same time as these secular experiments. There was Andreas Bernardus Smilnikar, an Austrian professor, who ' perceived that the signs of the times corresponded with the prophecies of the Bible, and that the time was at hand for the foundation of the universal peace which was promised to all nations'. Acting on this idea he went to America in 1838, and travelled over the country announcing that he was ' the Ambassador Extraordinary of Christ, and the Apostle of Peace'. He found people to believe him, and presently established a small German-speaking colony called the Peace Union settlement, which lasted for nearly a year.

In 1852 a Second Adventist preacher named Peter Armstrong made an attempt to lead 144,000 saints into the Wilderness to await the coming of the Lord. He bought 2500 acres of stony land in the Alleghenny Mountains, deeded the land to God with all the legal formalities available in the State, named it 'Celesta', and settled there with his wife and seven children. Instead of working the land, which in view of the immanent end of the world was hardly necessary, he edited a newspaper, 'The Day Star of Zion', which he claimed had thousands of readers ; and as the years went on a few foolish people really did join him in his retreat. Quarrels arose, however, and he was accused of being crazy ; and some of his supporters turned against him, and exposed his errors in the other Second Adventist papers (of which there were three or four in the 'sixties) and gradually they all drifted away from him. After his death his sons had some difficulty in claiming the land, because of the deed of gift which Peter Armstrong had executed ; but ultimately they succeeded, and all traces of Celesta faded away.

These isolated and pathetic attempts to inaugurate a new era were of little general interest at the time, and are still less important now ; but the Swedenborgian Spiritualist Movement of the same date was much more considerable, and had a recognizable influence upon the thought of the period.

One of the necessities of a movement in the United States, if it was to attract American adherents, was that it should appear to be either of native origin or so much modified and improved by transportation to America as to be as good. Owen, indeed, had been able to make no such pretence, but his enthusiastic admiration for the country and all its institutions perhaps did as well ; and the Fourierites, though they were following a

Frenchman, quickly lost sight of him, and replaced him by leaders of their own. The Abolitionists, though friendly with their English compeers, were not influenced by them, and made no use in their propaganda of the practical example of Great Britain ; and indeed they were aware that the triumph of Abolition in the British Empire, if it had any influence in America at all, was as likely to harden opposition as to win friends. England was wonderfully unpopular in the United States after the war of 1812 and there was no inclination to follow in her footsteps.

Exactly the same situation arose in regard to Swedenborgianism. There were, it is true, a number of New Jerusalem churches preaching the orthodox Swedenborgian faith ; but they were small and unimportant, and very largely confined to the Scandinavian immigrants. The religion made no stir and attracted no attention at all until an American prophet arose to call it to life.

The prophet was an uneducated cobbler of Poughkeepsie, N.Y., who went by the thoroughly American name of Andrew Jackson Davis. He abandoned cobbling for the profession of medical clairvoyant which he learnt by a simple method. ' By looking through space directly into Nature's laboratory ', he said, ' I easily acquired the common (and even the Greek and Latin) names of the various medicines, and also of many parts of the human structure.' With this equipment he did pretty well, but at some date before 1847 his views were enlarged by acquaintance with the works of Swedenborg—or more probably

of some garbled and summarized version of those works
—which took a firm hold on his imagination. The
teachings of Swedenborg are difficult and obscure
enough in themselves. His system of cosmogony, his
complex theology, and his mysterious doctrine that
every natural object is the expression of spiritual facts
have caused much confusion, and his doctrine that
the union of male and female is the motive of all celestial
facts, leading on as it does to the doctrine of counterparts, and the probable imperfection of human marriages,
has given rise to much trouble. Swedenborg's practice
of 'internal respiration', whatever it may have been
in the Master, has been indistinguishable from epilepsy
in some of his followers, and nothing in his creed has
been completely intelligible except his rejection of the
authority of St. Paul. Andrew Jackson Davis, however,
found no difficulty in absorbing the whole thing ; and
though he certainly got it wrong, that did not trouble
him at all. He felt that he was inspired upon his own
account, and he began to give vent to prophetic utterances and dark sayings. This in itself would have been
of little importance. There were doubtless innumerable
humble people uttering strange nonsense in various
parts of the United States, and no one was much the worse.
But the Seer of Poughkeepsie was destined for a more
exalted fate.

Albert Brisbane, the disappointed Fourierite leader,
heard of his existence, and Professor Bush, the leading
exponent of real Swedenborgianism went to see him.
Both these men were eager to be convinced ; and

before long they were engaged in alternate sessions taking down from dictation the inspired sayings of the cobbler.

By this method of joint authorship four immense volumes were produced, which were called ' The Great Harmonia', and put forth with a flourish of trumpets to astonish the world. 1847 was the right year for this publication. The special public which had been excited by the previous movements was still in a state of eager uncertainty about the truth ; the cloud of civil war, though it might be seen upon the horizon was not so near as to distract men's minds from their religious preoccupations, and no other rival held the field. ' The Great Harmonia', therefore, had an immense success, and its author was hailed as the greatest writer of America, and the most inspired teacher of all time. Davis, a little unsettled by so much praise, kept his inspiration moving. He speedily ' outgrew ' his master, and plunged off, unaided, into the realms of Spiritualism, where he finally foundered and sank. For a while he preached a grand mixture of intuition, free love, astronomical theology, ghostly spheres, familiarity between the living and the dead, the double sex of the Deity, and the divine harmonies of true marriage ; then he added an attack on medicine, a belief in animal magnetism and satanic arts, and finally, dancing, prophesying, and wrapt in his visions, he disappeared from view to pass in the end, into that other world he had so wildly imagined, and to seek there, perhaps, for the ghostly company he had evoked on earth.

The impetus which Spiritualism received from this mountebank prophet by no means passed away with his personal influence. All over the countryside simple people began to see ghosts, and mediums of every kind made their appearance. The famous Fox sisters, Kate and Maggie, inaugurated the era of ' rappings ' at Rochester in 1850, and although they later confessed that the strange noises which followed them about were produced by the cracking of their own toes inside their own boots, nothing so prosaic could check the movement. Conjurors, mesmerists and possessors of second sight sprang up on every hand, and the practice of necromancy returned. The age-old longing of mankind to penetrate the mystery of death set the feet of the people in strange ways, and credulity slipped over the bounds of reason, and opened the gates to madness and imposture of every kind. Nothing checked the mania, where once it had found a place. Every kind of ingenious sophistry was invoked to explain away discrepancies and failures, Secret and adverse forces were thought to be at work ; evil spirits were masquerading as divine ; the revelations, in themselves grotesquely absurd, were thought to be scattered portions of messages which the spirits of the dead were prevented from fully revealing. Mesmerists, and all the tribe of healers, mediums and phrenologists received new encouragement, and magnetic fluids, electric healing machines and magical devices were sold in great numbers. Automatic writing produced a great crop of literature, and table turning, mysterious touches in the darkness, angelic visitations, and plain old-fashioned ghosts appeared on every side.

It is interesting to notice that an outbreak of Spiritualism among the Shakers had preceded the Swedenborgian approach by several years. Between 1837 and 1844, that is to say at the time when the Fourierite Movement was beginning, the Shakers were attacked by a horde of spirits who tried to find expression through their mouths. These excellent and simple people firmly believed that the spirits were real, and they took the manifestations to which they were subject as the first stirrings of the end of the world, and were convinced that some wonderful ' afflatus ' would pass out from their own Society and spread over the Universe. They had, however, enough sense to realize that the strange things the spirits drove them to say and do would be regarded as ' unadulterated foolishness ' by the outside world, and in consequence they closed their doors to strangers, and admitted no one to their meetings during all that time. One of their temporary members, however, has left a record which is so quaint and strange, and in its way so touching, that it deserves to be remembered.

' To enable you to understand these scenes', he writes, ' I must give you as near as I can the ideas the Shakers have of the other world. Heaven is a Shaker Community on a very large scale. Everything in it is spiritual. Jesus Christ is the Head Elder, and Mother Ann the Head Eldress. The buildings are large and splendid, being all of white marble. There are large orchards with all kinds of fruit . . . but all is spiritual. Outside of this Heaven the spirits of the departed wander about on the surface of the earth (which is the Shaker Hell) till they are converted to Shakerism. Spirits are sent out on missionary tours, to preach to the wandering ones until they profess the faith, and then they are admitted. . . . On the dancing days . . . the brothers formed a rank on the right, the sisters on the left, facing each other about five feet apart. After all were in their proper places the chief Elder stepped into the centre of the space, and gave an exhortation for about five minutes, concluding with the invitation to them all to " go forth, old men, young men and maidens, and worship God with all their might in the dance." Accordingly they went forth, the men stripping off their coats and remaining in their shirt sleeves. First they formed a procession and marched around the room at double-quick time, while four brothers and sisters stood in the centre singing for them. After marching in this manner until they got a little warm they commenced dancing, and continued until they were all pretty well tired. During the dance the sisters kept on one side and the brothers on the other, and not a word was spoken by any of them. After they appeared to have had enough of this exercise the Elder gave the signal to stop, when each one took his or her place in an oblong circle formed around the room, and all waited to see if anyone had received a "gift", that is, an inspiration to do something odd. Then two of the sisters would commence whirling around like a top, with their eyes shut. . . . During this whirl the members stood round like statues, looking on in solemn silence. On some occasions, when a sister had stopped her whirling she would say, " I have a communication to make ", when the head Eldress would step to her side and receive the communication, and then make known the nature of it to the community. The first message I heard was as follows : " Mother Ann has sent two angels to inform us that a tribe of Indians has been round here two days, and wants the brothers and sisters to take them in. They are outside the building there, looking in at the windows ". I shall never forget how I looked round, expecting to see the yellow faces when this announcement was made. It caused no alarm to the rest, but the first Elder exhorted the brothers to " take in the poor spirits and assist them to get salvation ". After this we dispersed to our separate bedrooms, with the hope of having a future entertainment for the Indians. The next dancing night we again assembled as before, and went through the marching and dancing as usual, after which the hall doors were opened, and the Elder invited the Indians to come in. The doors were soon shut again, and one of the sisters (the same who had received the original communication) informed us that she saw Indians all around and among the brothers and sisters. The Elder then urged upon the members the duty of "taking them in ", whereupon eight or nine sisters became possessed of the spirits of Indian squaws, and about six of the brethren became Indians. Then ensued a regular pow-wow, with whooping and yelling and strange antics. . . . The sisters and brothers squatted down on the floor together, Indian fashion, and the Elders and Eldresses endeavoured to keep them asunder, telling the men they must be separated from the squaws, and otherwise instructing them in the rules of Shakerism. . . . These performances continued till about ten o'clock ; then the chief Elder requested the Indians to go away, telling them they would find someone waiting to conduct them to the Shakers in the heavenly world. At this announcement the possessed men and women became themselves again, and all retired to rest.

' At one of the meetings . . . it was revealed to us that Mother Ann was present, and that she had brought a dozen baskets of spiritual fruit for her children ; upon which the Elder invited all to go forth to the baskets in the centre of the floor, and help themselves. Accordingly they all stepped forth and went through the motions of taking fruit and eating it. You will wonder if I helped myself to fruit like the rest. No ; I had not faith enough to see the baskets or the fruit ; and you may think perhaps that I laughed at the scene ; but in truth I was so much affected by the general gravity and the solemn faces I saw around me that it was impossible to laugh.

' Other things as well as fruit were sometimes sent as presents, such as spiritual golden spectacles. These heavenly ornaments came in the same way as the fruit, and just as much could be seen of them. . . . On the second Sunday I spent with the Shakers there was a curious exhibition. . . . After dinner all the members

assembled in the hall and sang two songs. Then the
Elder informed them that it was a " gift for them to
march in procession, with their golden instruments
playing as they marched, to the holy fountain, and wash
away all the stains that they had contracted by sinful
thoughts and feelings ; for Mother Ann was pleased
to see her children pure and holy". I looked for the
musical instruments, but as they were spiritual I could
not see them. The procession marched two and two
into the yard and round the square, and came to a halt
in the centre. During the march each one made a
sound with the mouth, to please him or herself, and at
the same time went through the motions of playing on
some particular instrument, such as the clarinet, the
French horn, trombone, bass-drum, etc. ; and such a
noise was made that I felt as if I had got among a band
of lunatics. Most of the brethren then commenced
going through the motions of washing face and hands,
but finally some of them tumbled themselves in all
over ; that is they rolled on the grass, and went through
comical and fantastic capers. . . .

'During my whole stay with the Shakers a revival
was going on among the spirits in the invisible world
. . . and much of the members' time was spent in such
performances. It appeared to me that whenever any of
the brethren or sisters wanted to have some fun they
got possessed of spirits. . . . I might occupy great
space if I were to go into details of these spiritual performances ; but there was so much similarity in them
that I must ask the reader to let the above suffice.'

These queer and innocent manifestations did not spread outside the Shaker villages, and after a time the impulse to create them died away. The brethren and sisters perhaps found other ways of amusing themselves, or grew tired of their peculiar gifts. At any rate, the revival among the spirits in the invisible world did not last beyond 1844, and by the time that the Seer of Poughkeepsie arose, the Shakers had returned to their normal quietness, and were uninterested in his visions.

His movement was neither so short lived nor so unsuccessful as its predecessors, and in 1865, eighteen years after it had begun, a grand Convention of Spiritualists was held in Chicago. It was claimed that the belief had three million adherents, and there were certainly innumerable flourishing newspapers and a vast literature as well as a swarm of practitioners. 'The old religion is dying out,' they claimed. 'We represent the new, born of the Union of the types of humanity in a cosmopolitan geography, the die of which was cast in the Forges of Divine Providence.' Whatever this may mean, it hardly seems to have been a true claim ; for the old religion is still predominant in America.

Among the protagonists of the Spiritualism of the 'fifties and 'sixties were Robert Dale Owen and Frances Wright. These two, after the collapse of their colonies at New Harmony and Nashoba, collaborated in publishing a paper called the 'Free Enquirer', and in lecturing extensively over the country on free love, Abolition, Spiritualism and female emancipation. Although they made public speeches about free love, they gave no real cause for the scandals which everywhere accompanied them. In spite of their principles they both married in the ordinary way, Frances Wright married a Frenchman, Phiquepal d'Arusmont, who had been at New Harmony, and Robert Dale Owen married Mary Robinson. He wrote and published a book called 'Moral Physiology', which dealt with problems of population and birth control, and which was profoundly shocking at the time. He remained convinced of the truth of his Spiritualist ideas, but did not succeed in founding any sort of a school, and in later life he became deeply immersed in politics in which he was very successful. He was elected first to the State Legislature, and then to the Senate as a Democrat, and finally appointed Ambassador to Naples. His daughter, Rosamund, followed his Spiritualistic faith, and we shall meet her again in another, though a similar, connexion.

We need not follow the course of Spiritualism beyond this point. With the appearance of Mme. Blavatsky, the Purple Mother and the Theosophical Movement it became a different movement ; and it is to this day a living faith with adherents in all parts of the world.

It is worth nothing, however, that the early stages of American Spiritualism were closely connected with Faith Healing and Higher Thought. Andrew Jackson Davis was 'a medical clairvoyant' before he became a prophet, and his disturbed and incoherent doctrines did much to encourage the atmosphere in which, a few

years later, Mary Baker Eddy found her first adherents.
Christian Science, like Theosophy, is a living belief, and
one which has built up a vast and powerful edifice in
the modern world.   Its origin, however, lay among
obscure and ignorant people in the confused decades of
the middle of the nineteenth century ; and although it
is not suitable to describe it here, it was clearly a religion
parallel and comparable to those we are describing.

CHAPTER VII

THE PERFECTIONISTS OF ONEIDA

I N the foregoing chapter we have seen something of
the credulous attitude of religious and idealistic
people in the United States in the first half of the nineteenth century, and the peculiar and adventurous atmosphere in which they lived. It remains to describe in
more detail the two most extreme examples of abnormal
religions, the Perfectionists of Oneida and the Brotherhood of the New Life.

The leaders of these two sects, John Humphrey
Noyes (1811–1886) and Thomas Lake Harris (1823–
1903), were both of them educated men, and men of
great personal charm. Both were earnest and sincere
Christians in their youth, and both honestly believed
themselves to be the recipients of Divine inspiration.
Both led their followers to believe remarkable delusions,
and both were forced by the pressure of outside public
opinion to abandon their strange practices before they
died ; and both, in their curious courses through life,
completely and thoroughly dislocated the lives of those
with whom they came in contact.

We must consider them separately, taking Noyes, the
earliest in date, and the least dangerous in practice, first.

When the great Revival of 1831 swept over the New
England States, John Humphrey Noyes was a young

man of twenty. He was caught up in the enthusiasm of the great awakening, and as he himself said, ' Fixed his heart on the millennium, and resolved to live or die for it'. Being by nature thoughtful and independent, and not in the least afraid of following his own ideas to what seemed to him their logical consequences, he was soon in a heretical position. He studied theology at Andover, and at Yale, and read the Bible so repeatedly, and so attentively that to the end of his life he could name not only the book and chapter, but even the number of the verse and the place on the page of almost every text submitted to him. During the course of these studies he made a discovery which altered his whole outlook on life, and which separated him at once from the orthodox Churches. This discovery was that the Second Advent had already taken place, at the time of the fall of Jerusalem in the year A.D. 70, and he understood from this that the Devil had at that moment begun his reign, and that the symptom of his power was the existence of the organised Churches. The Ten Commandments, he thought, had at that same moment ceased to be in force, and consequently all that was needed for Salvation was a full consecration and a genuine belief. Upon those who could achieve these things the mantle of perfection would descend, and thereafter they would be incapable of sin.

Noyes himself reached this enviable position on the 20th of February, 1834 ; and from that moment, while he and his followers considered that he was perfect, the world at large held that he was crazy.

The immediate result of this revelation was the foundation of a small new sect which was called the Perfectionist or Pauline Church. Its first adherents were Noyes's own family : his mother, his brother and sisters, with their various husbands and wives. This small group gathered at Putney, Vermont, and John Humphrey devoted the greater part of his time and money to writing and printing books and pamphlets in which his views were set forth. By degrees others were attracted by his writings, and isolated Perfectionists appeared in various places, though none of them were very successful in persuading their neighbours that they were without sin. The most sincere of the new converts were George and Mary Cragin, who came into the faith through many trials, and whose pitiful love story is told by Hepworth Dixon in ' Spiritual Wives'. George adored Mary his wife to such an extent that he feared it was idolatry ; and Mary felt it was her duty to become the spiritual wife of one of the Perfectionist preachers whose real wife was distasteful to him. The tangle which the four of them got into would be familiar enough, were it not for the complication of motives which their inability to sin introduced ; and it seems that they were only rescued from it by the personal intervention of Noyes himself. He may have been crazy, as people said ; but he had plenty of common sense ; and after they came under his wing the course of the Cragins seems to have run smooth.

Whether it was this episode, or some other impulse

connected with his own life, or merely the effect of pure reason, illuminated from Heaven, a new doctrine appeared among the Perfectionists not long after this time (1845), namely, the doctrine of 'complex marriage'. It was the period of the Fourier Phalanxes, and Noyes, who was of an enquiring turn of mind, was watching them closely. He saw them fail, one after another, and wondered what was the cause. He was convinced that communism was the Apostolic design for society, and refused to attribute their disasters to this cause ; and at last, after studying the Scriptures with this problem in view, he grew convinced that their root trouble was the exclusiveness involved in the ordinary conception of sexual love and marriage. ' The new commandment is that we love one another, and that not by pairs, but *en masse*. We are required to love one another fervently ; the fashion of the world forbids a man and a woman who are otherwise appropriated to love one another fervently, but if they obey Christ they must do this.' It seemed perfectly obvious and clear. From this premise Noyes built up a remarkable superstructure, and he made no secret of it, but described it in the plainest terms. ' Love is not a sin,' he said. ' Susceptibility to love is not burnt out by one honeymoon or satisfied with one love. On the contrary, the more you do the more you can. It is the law of Nature.'

No one could misunderstand this, it would seem ; and when he presently announced that his people at Putney were putting it into practice, a great scandal arose. Noyes and his followers were chased away from the place, with threats of tarring and feathering, and were forced to settle elsewhere. John Humphrey moved to Oneida, New York, in 1847, and the whole group had followed him by 1849, and settled together into a community which for many years attracted attention and excited curiosity far and wide.

The Oneida Community published an immense amount of literature, including annual reports, weekly and bi-weekly newspapers, books, pamphlets and short articles. There was no obscurity as to their beliefs or their way of living, and nothing whatever in the nature of a hidden doctrine. Nor, except for the main basis of their family life, was there any scandal attaching to the place. The members of the Community lived in peace with each other. They neither quarrelled nor left, and they professed themselves happy and contented. They prospered, in the worldly sense, and made a great deal of money, and there seems to have been no question of disobedience or disloyalty among them. From 1847, when the Community began, until 1881, when at Noyes's own suggestion their peculiar system of marriage was abandoned, no trouble of any kind seems to have arisen from within, and no flaw to have appeared in the working out of their theories.

The secret of their success, of course, lay in the personality of John Humphrey, their leader. He managed the temporal and the spiritual and the domestic affairs of his large family with an iron hand, and at the same time he used so much good sense and so much tact in detail, that the crookedest paths became straight, and the wildest contradictions credible under his rule. But to those who did not fall under his sway it remains exceedingly difficult, to say the least, to believe that he was acting on the right lines, or that the system he upheld was anything but the wildest nonsense.

It is worth while to examine the philosophy of John Humphrey Noyes in some detail, for it presents some quite unusual features, and abounds in instructive parallels. And moreover the Community in which the philosophy was put into practice was so amusing, and at the same time so prosperous, that it affords the one pleasant picture in the whole course of our story, and seems to make a kind of gleam of brightness amid the sordid tragedies of abnormal religious experiments.

After the purely theological belief in the dual sex of the Almighty, which Noyes shared with the Shakers and the Swedenborgians, and the purely historical belief that the Second Coming had already arrived, the cardinal point in the Perfectionist faith was the possibility of personal sinlessness. This belief, in itself very old, has tended to reappear in persecuted and fanatical sects all through the ages, as for example among the Euchites of the fifth and sixth centuries, and the Cathari or Eastern Manicheans of the twelfth and thirteenth. The Inner Circle of initiates of these last were actually called 'Perfecti', and similar claims were made at Munster during the wild year when the Anabaptists believed it to be the New Jerusalem. In all these cases, however, extreme asceticism, or extreme licentiousness marked the professors of sinlessness. They either avoided the world, and so left the possibility of sin behind them, or they claimed that nothing was wrong if they did it.

The followers of Noyes, however, adopted neither of these positions. It is true that they constructed a world of their own, in which special laws prevailed, and that they adopted a highly peculiar system of sex morality. But they were neither ascetic nor licentious, but on the contrary strictly practical and severely disciplined. Their belief may have been, perhaps, the descendant of the old faiths ; but their interpretation of it was peculiar to themselves.

Communism of goods was another of the main features of the Perfectionist school, and this, as we have seen, was a very common method of interpreting the Scriptures. As in his sinlessness, so in his Communism, however, Noyes introduced an original note. There must be communism not only in goods, but also in affections. The separate husband or wife, and the individual family were the negation of the doctrine in his eyes ; and accordingly they were cast out.

Group marriage is said to have existed among some of the earliest known tribes of men, and occasional minor instances of it come from time to time before the courts ; but as a religious system it seems to have no parallel, and to be the unique product of Oneida. In the year A.D. 97, indeed, Bishop Clement, one of the personal disciples of the Apostles, became jealous of his wife, and on being reproved for this fault he brought her to the assembly and offered her to anyone who wanted her. His idea was said to have been that the flesh must be abused ; but this doctrine, which was ascetic in intention (at any rate as far as the Bishop himself was concerned) was very soon perverted, as can be imagined, and lost its original force.

The idea of abusing the flesh was in any case foreign to the Perfectionists. Their aims were definitely practical, and the inspiration of their attempt to control and subjugate the passions was more directly due to sociological than to religious convictions. Noyes held that excessive child-bearing was a curse which should be lifted from woman as she reached the true Church, and he devised and made strong propaganda for methods by which it might be avoided. He did not believe, like Simon Magnus the Gnostic, that the procreation of children was the work of Satan ; he did not, like the Khylisti, call babies 'little sins', nor exalt celibacy. On the contrary he arranged very carefully for the reproduction of his community, and selected the men and women who were to play their parts in the affair. But what he did require, and apparently obtain, was the subordination of their passions to his orders, and a general acceptance of the idea that partners should at once be changed when symptoms of violent or ' selfish ' affection began to appear.

There was one other belief which the Perfectionists translated into practical terms, and that was the belief that all diseases are of diabolical origin. This, of course, was by no means the exclusive discovery of John Humphrey Noyes. The Shakers thought the same, and so did the Christian Scientists, who were in a few years to gather about Mrs. Eddy. It is one of the oldest beliefs of mankind, dating far beyond the Christian era ; and the Gnostics of the first and second centuries only carried on a tradition which was already firmly established.

John Humphrey, however, treated this subject, as he did the others, in an original way. He did not trust in exorcism, nor in magic ; he did not try to enlist angels on his side, nor even rely upon the unaided powers of the mind. His plan was described by himself in 1863, and his own words will make it clear.

' It is a common custom here for every one who may be attacked with any disorder to apply this remedy, by sending for a committee of six or eight persons in whose faith and spiritual judgment he has confidence to come and criticize him. The result, when administered sincerely, is almost universally to throw the patient into a sweat, or to bring on a reaction of his life against disease, breaking it up, and restoring him soon to usual health. We have seen this result produced without any other agency except the use of ice in perhaps twenty cases of sore throat within a few weeks, We have seen it take effect at an advanced stage of chronic disease, and raise a person up apparently from death's door. It seems a somewhat heroic method of treatment when a person is suffering in body to apply a castigation of the character through the spiritual or moral part ; but this is precisely the thing needed to cleanse and purify the system from disease. We have tried it and found it to be invaluable. To all who have faith in Christ as a physician we can commend this prescription. If you are sick, seek for some one to tell you your faults, to find out your weakest spot in character or conduct ; let them put their finger on the very sore that you would best like to keep hid. Depend upon it, *there* is the avenue through which disease gets access to you. And if the sincerity which points this out and opens it to the light hurts, and is mortifying for the time being, it is only a sign that the remedy is applied at the right place, and is taking effect.'

There is a mixture of shrewdness and innocence about this medicine which typifies the whole outlook of Oneida. Noyes and his followers did not pause to criticize their own thinking, or attempt to test it against anything more universal than their immediate observation. They acted in absolute good faith, and published their conclusions in all earnestness ; for they were quite sure that they were right.

The men and women who accepted this mass of queer doctrine lived together in one large dwelling under the autocratic rule of their prophet. They led a very easy and pleasant life, and devoted much intelligence to making themselves comfortable. The work was distributed evenly, and not too arduously among them, and all the latest labour-saving appliances were installed. There was a library which was greatly used, and a good school for the children, who, when they were old enough were sent on (both boys and girls) to Yale and Cornell and other colleges. Games and musical gatherings were encouraged, and croquet was an especial favourite. On the shores of Oneida lake, twelve miles away, there was a summer house, where the members went for fishing and boating and bathing, and they were called upon to face none of the austerities and self-denials of the other community experiments, and did not even disturb themselves to observe the Sabbath in any special way. They had excellent meals and varied their routine widely, sometimes having three and sometimes eight meals a day. The women, who were in all respects on an equality with the men, wore a special costume consisting of long trousers covered by short tunics, and cut off their hair. Goldwin Smith, who visited the place in 1874 records his opinion that it was highly unbecoming, but the pictures which have been preserved do not bear this out.

They admired their own method of dressing, but were not bigoted about it, and maintained that they were open to new lights, ' the last thing not yet having been done in the way of hats and boots'.

In spite of all the pleasantness and variety of their lives, however, the members were under a strict discipline, and their inner thoughts, even more than their outward actions, were subject to the authority of their ruler. They were expected to give a full and free account of themselves, and to seek permission before entering into any of the special alliances which it was their religious duty to contract, and all proposals were made, somewhat formally, in the presence of a third party. Noyes held that it was best, as a rule, for affinities to spring up between men and women of different ages, and he paired off his people, the younger men with the older women, and *vice versa*. When it was desired that the unions should lead to the birth of children this rule was not always observed ; but Noyes was careful to separate the couple again, before too long a time had passed, lest the insidious evil of exclusive affection should find its way in. In the same way, although the mothers were allowed to care for their own infants, they were not allowed to have sole charge, and if they showed too great a devotion they were gently led to other ways. The temper of the whole group, even when in health, was kept in periodic order by the institution of Criticism, an exercise which Noyes greatly admired. This ceremony consisted in the public discussion of the character of one of the community, who volunteered for the post, and who was obliged to sit in silence while the others dealt faithfully with all his faults and failings. No better idea of the working of this remarkable institution can be given than by quoting an account, left by an eye-witness, which is all the more interesting in that it reveals, by the way, the general tone and temper of the place.

' On Sunday afternoon, by the kindness of a young man who had offered himself for criticism, I was permitted to be present. Fifteen persons besides myself, about half women, and about half young people under thirty, were seated in a room, mostly on benches placed against a wall. Among them was Mr. Noyes himself, who sat in a large rocking chair. The young man to be criticized, whom I will call Charles, sat inconspicuously in the midst of the company. When the doors were closed he was asked by the leader (not Mr. Noyes) whether he desired to say anything. Retaining his seat he said he had suffered for some time past from certain intellectual difficulties and doubts—a leaning especially towards Positivism, and a lack of faith ; being drawn away from God ; a tendency to think religion of small moment. But that he had combated the evil spirit within him, and he hoped he had gained somewhat ; and so on.

Hereupon a man being called upon to speak, remarked that he thought Charles had been somewhat hardened by too great good fortune, that his success in certain enterprises had somewhat spoiled him ; that he was somewhat wise in his own esteem ; not given to consult with others, or to seek to take advice. One or two other men gave examples to show these faults. Another concurred in the general testimony, but added that he thought Charles had lately made efforts to correct some of his faults, though there was still much room for improvement.

A young woman next remarked that Charles was haughty and supercilious, and thought himself better than others ; that he spoke needlessly curt to those with whom he had to speak. Another young woman added that Charles was a respecter of persons ; that he showed his liking for certain individuals too plainly by calling them pet names before people ; that he seemed to forget that such things were disagreeable and wrong.

Another woman said that Charles was often careless in his language. Also that he did not always conduct himself at table, especially before visitors, with careful politeness and good manners.

A man concurred in this, remarking that he had heard Charles condemn a beefsteak as tough, and make other unnecessary remarks about the food while he was eating.

Another said that Charles, though industrious and faithful in all temporalities, and a very able man, was not religious at all. A man remarked that Charles was, as others had said, somewhat spoiled by his own success, but that it was a mistake for him to be so, for he was certain that Charles's success came mainly from the wisdom and care with which the society had surrounded him with good advisers who had guided him ; and that Charles ought therefore to be humble, instead of proud and haughty, as one who ought to look outside of himself for the real sources of his success.

Finally two or three remarked that he had been in a certain transaction insincere toward another young man, saying one thing to his face and another to others ; and in this one or two women concurred.

Amid all this very plain speaking, which I have here considerably condensed, Charles sat speechless, looking before him ; but as the accusations multiplied his face grew paler, and drops of perspiration began to stand on his forehead. The remarks I have reported took up about half an hour ; and now, each one in the circle having spoken, Mr. Noyes summed up.

113

He said that Charles had some serious faults ; that he had watched him with some care, and that he thought the young man was earnestly trying to cure himself. He spoke in general praise of his ability, his good character, and of certain temptations he had resisted in the course of his life. He thought he saw signs that Charles was making a real and earnest attempt to conquer his faults ; and as one evidence of this he remarked that Charles had lately come to him to consult him upon a difficult case in which he had had a severe struggle, but had in the end succeeded in doing right. ' In the course of what we call stirpiculture,' said Noyes, ' Charles as you know, is in the situation of one who is by and by to become a father. Under these circumstances, he has fallen under the too common temptation of selfish love, and a desire to wait upon and cultivate an exclusive intimacy with the woman who is to bear a child through him. This is an insidious temptation, very apt to attack people under such circumstances ; but it must nevertheless be struggled against.' Charles, he went on to say, had come to him for advice in this case, and he (Noyes) had at first refused to tell him anything, but had asked him what he thought he ought to do. That after some conversation Charles had determined, and he had agreed with him, that he ought to isolate himself entirely from the woman, and let another man take his place at her side, and this Charles had accordingly done, with a most praiseworthy spirit of self-sacrifice. Charles indeed had still further taken up his cross, as he had noticed with pleasure, by going to sleep with the smaller children, to take charge of them during the night. Taking all this in view, he thought Charles was in a fair way to become a better man, and had manifested a sincere desire to improve, and to rid himself of all his selfish faults.

Thereupon the meeting was dismissed.

Under such rules and discipline the Community at Oneida lived and flourished from 1847 to 1879, and set up branch establishments at Wallingford and at Putney (from whence they had come). During all this time they excited the greatest curiosity, and received innumerable visitors from all over the world, as many as five hundred coming to see them in a single month. Although their beliefs and practices were well understood, no active opposition made its appearance. Many indeed condemned their system ; no one save themselves defended it ; but they were liked by their neighbours, and their increasing prosperity made them widely esteemed. This prosperity came, in the first instance, from the making of traps. ' The Earth', Noyes said, ' is lying under a curse of Vermin, and the Saints must make war and destroy '. The trap business brought in an immediate return, and the Community then set up a fruit canning factory, which, though it commanded no such exalted sanction, was an equally great commercial success.

In 1873, however, in spite of the prosperity and the general harmlessness of the community, the Presbyterian Synod of Central New York took the field against them, and a clerical persecution on a large scale was begun, which led, in 1879, to the holding of a special Convention on the subject of Oneida at Syracuse. A campaign of this kind, once set on foot, gathers momentum without difficulty, and John Humphrey watched its progress with anxiety. Had the time now come, he wondered, to remove the rock of offence, namely complex marriage, and so secure to his people an undisturbed future ? He realized that he was an old man ; he knew that the young people whom he had educated in the world outside were less tolerant of his authority, and less certain of his inspiration than their fathers and mothers ; and, after much heart-searching he decided to bow to the storm.

' I propose,' he announced in August, 1879, ' that we give up the practice of Complex Marriage, not as renouncing belief in the principle and prospective finality of that institution, but in deference to the public sentiment which is evidently rising against it.' This proposal was accepted by the whole Community six days later, not without heart-burning and distress, but in the same perfect good faith as had characterized them throughout. Those who had been legally married when they entered the Community resumed their original state ; those who were still legally unmarried nearly all selected permanent partners, and less than six of the whole number (at that time nearly two hundred) preferred a celibate life.

The break up of the single family into separate families did not at first alter the way of life of the Community, but Noyes and his assistants realized that it would be likely to introduce difficulties before long.

In 1881 therefore they decided to alter their form of common property, and became a regular Joint Stock Company, allotting the shares to the members in proportions agreed upon among them. Each adult member, without regard to sex or usefulness, received $100 in shares for every year they had been members, and in addition shares representing half the money they had originally brought in to the common stock. The children were guaranteed education, and $200 when they reached the age of sixteen ; and the old people could, if they preferred, accept annuities of $200 a year instead of their proportion of shares.

This division of the property was agreed to by all the members, and was carried out without the slightest trouble, and the Company (of which Noyes continued to be the Director until his death) prospered and did well. After a time, as Noyes had foreseen, the separate families scattered, though for many years they continued to come back to Oneida for their holidays, and kept in friendly touch with each other. But with the cessation of Complex Marriage the real experiment ended. When Noyes died his son succeeded to the management of the Company, with a regular Board of Directors, and although in 1907 it still had some communistic features, unlike those of ordinary commercial concerns, all traces of its religious character seemed to have left it, and as a sect it was completely at an end.

CHAPTER VIII

THE BROTHERHOOD OF THE NEW LIFE

THE story of the Community founded by Thomas Lake Harris, and of the strange religion invented and practised by him, is sadly different from the pleasant, if erratic, picture of Oneida. Everything connected with Harris is dark and mysterious, wrapped in a sort of esoteric symbolism, and enveloping a secret central doctrine which grows more and more repulsive the closer one approaches to understanding it. Moreover the prophet himself, as he stands revealed in the light of his words and actions, is not a shrewd and honest fellow, like John Humphrey Noyes, but a greedy and dangerous sensualist, self-deluded, no doubt, but arrogant, harsh and revengeful.

Harris was born in England, and taken to America by his parents in 1828, when he was five years old. From the age of nine he was obliged to support and educate himself, which he did with such success that by the time he was twenty-one he was a minister of the Fourth Universalist Church in New York City. Four years later he separated himself from that body, and became a preacher of an Independent Congregation, where his eloquence attracted wide celebrity. He was not only moving and impassioned in the pulpit, but also strikingly handsome, and, although there is no direct evidence upon the point, it is more than probable that the young man found himself the centre of an admiring and adoring group. This was the moment when ' The Great Harmonia ' was making its appearance, and Harris was profoundly impressed with some of the obscure doctrine enshrined within it. He began to write mystical and spiritualistic books and poems, and in 1851 he joined with J. L. Scott in a religious enterprise of a most peculiar nature. By means of ' rappings ' it was revealed to these two men that one of their friends, Ira. S. Hitchcock by name, had discovered the site of the Garden of Eden at Mountain Cove, Virginia. According to the revelation, no human foot had trodden this ground since the days of Adam and Eve ; the subsequent convulsions of nature had many times changed and altered the neighbouring country, but this sacred spot had remained untouched ; and in the near future, after they had built the ' City of Refuge ' there, these same convulsions were to be gone through backwards, and the earth was to return to its original state, everything except the Garden of Eden being destroyed. It was thus evident that only those who took shelter at Mountain Cove would escape the destruction accompanying the end of the world, and accordingly Scott, Harris, Hitchcock, and over a hundred followers set off for Virginia and established a community there.

Scott and Harris were both of them divinely inspired leaders of this movement. All the worldly goods of their adherents were made over to them (in trust, as they expressed it, for the Lord), and every command they issued had to be obeyed. Unfortunately, however, all did not go smoothly between the two prophets, and their inspired wishes clashed. In consequence of their disagreement revolts arose among their followers, some adhering to one and some to another, and the holy mountain became a scene of discord. The details of the disaster have not been preserved, but one band of fifty-three people withdrew, and then another followed suit, and finally the sacred spot was deserted. The Serpent scored his victory once more, and the ' dark cloud of magnetic death ' descended upon what was to have been the everlasting city.

Harris retired from the Garden of Eden (presumably with his share of the possessions which he was holding for the Lord), and became a leader of what was known as ' Christian Spiritualism '. He wrote a number of books whose meaning it is impossible to disentangle, in spite of the alluring terms in which his publishers announced them. ' These lyrics ', they wrote, ' with their introduction, are intended to declare some methods and processes whereby the Divine One-Twain Creator transposes the natural bodies of all such as receive and embody the Redemption-Life of the Saviour-Saviouress, from the separate sex-lines of the third dimension of con-dissolving nature, to those of the reunited twain-one sex of the fourth dimension of eternal Arch-Nature, whereby Sin is abolished in the flesh, and its wages, Death, abolished in and for the body.'[1] Whether this announcement caused the book to sell widely or to remain neglected it is impossible to tell ; but the chances seem to be in favour of neglect.

Harris travelled widely while he was writing these books, and working out the philosophy which he was later to put into practice. He spent several years in England, where he preached a sort of Swedenborgianism, and several in the Orient, where he learnt a strange vocabulary, and certain other things which mingled with his Swedenborgianism most harmoniously. He attracted, too, a number of scattered adherents, including some in Japan, and began to be recognized as the supreme prophet of a new and secret doctrine. After moving about from one place to another, and making at least one attempt at community life, he finally settled at Brocton, Salem on Erie, N.Y., where he opened the famous community of the Brotherhood of the New Life.

It is very difficult to give a coherent account of the beliefs which Harris taught, not because there is any lack of statements concerning them, but because these statements are one and all unintelligible. Harris published dozens of books, pamphlets, poems and sermons, some of them of great length ; but these do nothing but confuse the issue. They abound in esoteric language, in mystification and obscurity ; and even the grammar is so ' inspired ' that momentary gleams of meaning become lost in its mazes. A good many other people besides Harris himself have given accounts of the

[1] The Marriage of Heaven and Earth; Triumph of Life, by T. L. Harris. C. W. Pearce and Co., 139, Regent Street, Glasgow.

doctrines, however, and some attempt at restating them must here be made.

The belief was based, as so many others have been, upon the dual sex of the Almighty. From this basis it went on to maintain that man also, being created in the image of God, was a bi-sexual creature ; not, indeed, in this life, but in the fuller life towards which he must ever be striving. The necessary half needed to complete the full human being was called a Counterpart, who might possibly be met with on earth, and must certainly be searched for, but who would inevitably be met in Heaven if missed below.

This doctrine, which is, of course, at least as old as Plato, has always had an attraction for mankind. Whatever may be the intricacies and the complexities of mundane love, the possibility of an ideal union, amounting almost to identity between lovers, has shimmered before the eyes of mankind for long ages, and has inspired ecstacies, transports and disappointments without number.

In the Brotherhood of the New Life, however, little heed was paid to disappointments. The true counterpart could be approached through the false, and each person in whom you detected any noble and lovable quality was able, to that extent, to put you in touch with the real creature. Thus it was the duty of a true believer to love, and approach as close as possible to any and every other human being (if of the opposite sex), so as to be united to that part of their own counterpart which was mirrored within ; and the more often the experiment was repeated (with a different partner) the more thorough the approximation would become.

John Humphrey Noyes, who watched the Brocton experiment with great interest, remarked that this aspect of its teaching involved ' the delicate problems of the negative theory of chastity ' ; and indeed it did. Its implications can be readily understood, and need not be more explicitly stated. Certainly they were not clearly set forth by Harris, nor easily apprehended by his followers. For the doctrine of Counterparts, and the practice of union with partial counterparts, was the very innermost core of the sect. It was not revealed except to the most fully initiate, and to them only after years of preparation. Small and fugitive glimpses were allowed to be seen through the mass of verbiage and mystery ; hints and dark sayings, just sufficient to keep hope and curiosity alive, were meted out to the disciples, and occasionally, as the spirit moved the prophet, one or other of the female disciples would be taken behind the veil. But on the whole the Community at Brocton seems to have lived in ignorance of the exact terms of their high mission, and to have come only gradually to understand it.

They knew from the first that ' Father ', as they called Harris, had himself a female counterpart in Heaven. Her name was 'Lily Queen', and she, speaking through Harris, was destined to give the new revelations to the world. There was some confusion of thought here, as they undoubtedly sought to approach Harris's counterpart rather than their own in the first instance. But confusion of thought was a trifling difficulty in the Brotherhood of the New Life. Lily Queen, in any case, was the source of ' Father's ' inspiration ; and it was an honour even to know her name.

The belief in a female inspiration is perhaps as old as the idea of counterparts. In the Christian era it appears in the preachings of Simon Magnus, the first Gnostic preacher, who was himself adored as a god in Samaria in the first century. His ' Thought ', which was the source of his divinity, had been imprisoned for ages in one female body after another, that of Helen of Troy having been one. In the year 117 a disciple of his, Valentinus, revived the notion, maintaining that God had a wife, Sige (Silence), whose children, Intellect and Truth gave birth to the Word and Life, the Word being male, and Life female. At this point the doctrine of Valentinus swung off into an elaborate mythology of æons, leading to the Demiurge or Creator, and its resemblance to the teachings of Harris is only in its obscurity, and its suggestion that there are material men who must perish, and spiritual men who must be saved, and psychic men who may either perish or be saved according to the help they receive.

According to Harris one of the most important ways of getting help towards salvation was through the respiratory organs. He taught a system of ' internal respiration ' which resembled that of Swedenborg, and which all his disciples professed to be able to achieve. Man, said Harris, had no real life in himself ; it was only a divine 'inflowing', and by ' arch-natural ' breathing this inflowing could be enormously accelerated, and the whole substance of the body changed. Indeed towards the end Harris maintained that by this form of breathing old age and death itself could be defeated, and he claimed in his own person to have escaped all the disabilities natural to his years.

It is not necessary to try and give a reasonable description of the process, even if such a feat could be achieved. The description given by one of the practitioners, though it cannot be called reasonable, will be enough to explain the whole business.

' Internal Respiration may be briefly described thus,' he wrote.[1] ' It is breathing not only into the spirit, but also into the body, of the atmosphere of Heaven, the Divine Proceeding, or, as the Christian Church somewhat quaintly terms it, the Holy Ghost. It has therefore no relationship with the respiratory formulas of Occultism ; whether as taught secretly to the initiates of the Western and Eastern schools, the Rosicrucian and Theosophic Orders, or as partially revealed to the uninitiated as the Science of Breath. It is entirely on a different and a higher plane. These formulas of Occultism are in the Kabalistic world of ASSIAH, the plane of material action ; possibly, with a high adept, ascending to the world YETZIRAH, the angelic plane of formation, but scarcely beyond. Internal Respiration, on the other hand, commences in the world of ATZULITH,

---

[1] Internal Respiration, or the Plenary Gift of the Holy Spirit, by Respiro. E. W. Allen, 4, Ave Maria Lane, London, MDCCCXCVI. *Price* 2/-.

the Archetypical plane of pure Deity ; descending thence through the world BRIAH, the archangelic and creative plane ; till, passing through YETZIRAH, it is ultimated in ASSIAH. *From this it follows* (the italics are mine) that whereas the respiratory formulas of Occultism can be mastered by long practice combined with a determined will, Internal Respiration is a Divine Gift.'

Counterparts and internal respiration were the two great mysteries to which the community at Brocton was devoted, but there were also some practical aspects of the life which are worth consideration. The first of these was a sort of Communism, different indeed from that of the Owen or Fourier schools, though stoutly defended by the believers as being the same. In Harris's form of Communism all those who joined the Brotherhood made over to him without reserve all their worldly possessions. When this plan was criticized and questioned by the unfriendly the members boldly affirmed that they had done no such thing, though in fact, they had ; and they eased their consciences by the subterfuge that they had made over their goods to the Lord, and to ' Father ' only as His deputy. But the result, as far as the laws of the United States were concerned, was exactly the same ; and when trouble came it was in the courts that it had to be adjusted, and it was there that the true state of affairs was finally revealed.

Communism of goods, so adjusted, was accompanied by community of labour ; and here too ' Father ' ruled supreme. He was the owner of a considerable tract of land and a large business of grape growing, as well as several other enterprises which were carried on there. The members of the Community were required to work in these concerns, and to perform also all the necessary duties of the household ; and it was ' Father's ' custom to put new disciples on periods of severe probation, keeping them to strictly manual labour for as much as three or four years before he would allow them to penetrate any of the inner mysteries of the cult. The theory on which he said he based this probation was that work should take the place of mystical reveries, and that a preparation of this severe kind was in itself enough to prove the reality of the subsequent revelations. But it was noticeable that his own tests, and his own preparations were all over before the theory was evolved, and that his only personal contribution to the common toil was the writing of mystical books and the practical instruction of initiates into the secrets of counterparts.

Thomas Lake Harris was, at the time of his Brocton experiment, a most impressive and remarkable figure. His face was strikingly handsome, with deep-set, glowing eyes and a long white beard. His voice, which was a lovely one, was capable of extraordinary changes, as was his whole expression. He looked a prophet, and he adopted all the mannerisms most calculated to impress and overawe his companions, wrapping his movements in a cloud of secrecy, and making himself very difficult of access even to the faithful. He indulged in cryptic sayings, and in occasional, impassioned letters, and fascinated men and women by his obscure force. The most remarkable tribute to his power, and the most singular part of his history lies in his association with Laurence Oliphant which we must now describe.

Laurence Oliphant belonged to a well-known Scottish family, and was born in Ceylon in 1829, where his father was Chief Justice of the island. He was a brilliant and fascinating young man, whose love of adventure led him to all the troubled places of Europe to carry on unofficial missions and political journalism at the height of every crisis. He was in Southern Russia just before the Crimea, and then went on to join the British armies ; he was in China with Lord Elgin in 1857, and then went to America to examine the conditions in the South before the Civil War. In 1860 he was in Italy trying to help Cavour and Garibaldi, and a year later he was nearly killed in Japan, when he was acting as Secretary to the British Legation there. On his way home he met and travelled with the Prince of Wales' party, and in 1863 he rushed to Poland to take part in an insurrection there. The next year he was again in the thick of trouble, in Schleswig Holstein ; and wherever he went he contrived to write and send home brilliant and exciting articles, which were published sometimes by 'The Times', and sometimes in the 'Quarterly Reviews'. In 1864 he came back to London and plunged into society, where his connections, his brilliant talk and his fascinating personality made him an immediate favourite. The young man, indeed, seemed to have the whole of the great world at his feet, and nothing but his own waywardness gave any doubt that he would have a brilliant and distinguished career, either as a diplomat or as an author according to his choice.

The circumstances, and even the date when this favourite of fortune met the obscure American prophet are unknown ; but somewhere before 1860 they did meet, and the extraordinary influence of Harris began to show itself. Harris, indeed, was a preacher of new doctrines, known only to a handful of cranks, possessed of neither wealth nor influence. He lived at the other side of the world, and had no connexion with the young man's previous life ; yet after not more than half a dozen interviews he assumed complete control of Laurence Oliphant, and thenceforth for nearly fifteen years he dictated every action of his life.

He must have been in London in 1864, when Laurence returned there, for it was at this time that Laurence gave the first indications that he had abandoned his free will. The prophet's first orders were that he should continue where he was, and accordingly Laurence stood for, and was elected to, Parliament in 1865. Great things were expected of him. He was a good speaker, not at all shy or backward, and he had a knowledge of European politics which few men of twice his age could rival. He was extremely anxious to do well and hoped for a prosperous Parliamentary career. But his master, who had by then returned to America, had different designs. Orders came across the Atlantic that Laurence was not to speak in the House, and accordingly, to the surprise of everyone, the young man remained perfectly mute, and did not even make his maiden speech.

Two years went by thus ; and then in 1867 Laurence was called to Brocton and throwing over all his English life and his English friends he joined his master. The atmosphere into which he plunged in the little American community of thirty or forty people seems almost too fantastic for belief, and the account given in his ' Life ' by his cousin, Mrs. Oliphant, by no means exaggerates the facts. ' Many mediums ', she says, ' and possessed persons were brought to Harris, that he might cast out the devils by which they were afflicted. Sometimes the " infernals ", as they were called, were very active, and in that case the whole community had to watch to save those who were infested, because it was believed that the infernals were more active in sleep. For this reason, in many instances persons were kept almost without sleep for months. One woman in particular for weeks was allowed only to sleep from nine o'clock till twelve, all the rest of the twenty-four hours being spent in the hardest work. In casting out or " holding against " the devils, it was the custom to concentrate the mind firmly on the principle of evil, till it seemed almost to form itself into a definite form, and then to pray with frantic fervour, " Bind him, Lord ! " When the crisis was past, and the man or woman became open to spiritual influence, as betokened by deep sustained breathing, members used to sit up all night to " bind " the infernals ; it being understood that those who were most open to spiritual influence of the highest kind were also most subject to the other. . . . Harris arranged (his followers) in groups of three or four persons to assimilate ; but if the magnetism of one was found to be injurious to another, Harris was aware of it at once, and instantly separated them. Any strong, merely natural affection was injurious. In all such cases all ties of relationship were broken ruthlessly, and separations made between parents and children, husbands and wives, until " the affection was no longer selfish, but changed into a great spiritual love for the race ; so that, instead of acting and reacting on one another, it could be poured out on all the world, or at least on those who were in a condition to receive this pure spiritual love, to the perfection of which the most perfect harmony was necessary, any bickering or jealousy immediately dispelling the influx and " breaking the sphere ".'

While this mental struggle was going on, Laurence's body was equally hard worked. ' He was sent to sleep in a large loft, containing only empty orange boxes and one mattress. . . . His earliest work was clearing out a large cattle shed or stable. He often, he said, recalled in a sort of nightmare the gloomy, silent labour for days and days, wheeling barrows of dirt and rubbish in perfect loneliness, for he was not allowed to speak to anyone ; and even his food was conveyed to him by a silent messenger, to whom he might not speak a word. Often after this rough work was ended and he came home dead-beat at nine o'clock he was sent out again to draw water for household purposes till eleven o'clock, till his fingers were almost frost-bitten '.

Lady Oliphant followed her son to this community

in 1868, and was immediately set to work on her own probation, washing, cooking and cleaning for the household. To complete the ordeal she and her son were too much devoted to each other to be allowed to have any intercourse, and they were obliged to live as strangers side by side.

In 1869 Laurence's probation was over ; and then, without a word of leavetaking from his mother, he was sent back to his normal life in London, and told to carry on as before. He had made over all his money to Harris, and was now granted a small allowance, barely sufficient to live on, and ordered to send back to Brocton anything that he might make. This he did, and for the next two years, that is to say while he was acting as the ' Times ' correspondent in France during the war of 1870, every penny of his salary went back to Lake Erie to the upkeep of those who were fighting the devil upon its banks. In the midst of this work, and just at the most inconvenient moment, there came a sudden call to return ; and Laurence threw up everything once more and hurried to America. Presumably this call had been but a test, for he was allowed to return again almost at once, and settled in Paris, where his mother, her probation over, was also allowed to join him. And for a little space they lived there happily together, Laurence still working for the ' Times ', and still sending all his money to Harris.

In 1872 Laurence had to undergo another severe test. He met and fell in love with a young lady, as beautiful, as well connected, as brilliant and as charming as himself, and she fell in love with him. They wished to marry ; but before they could do so the permission of the distant ' Father ' on Lake Erie had to be obtained ; and it was very hard to get. Harris had to be assured that the new interest would not wean the disciple from the true path, and that Alice herself would accept his rule. He had to make sure that there would be no marriage settlements on either side ; that Alice's money would be freely made over to him, and that the whole of the relations between husband and wife would be under his control. A series of the most remarkable letters therefore passed to and fro across the Atlantic, of which the following extract, from a letter written by Alice to Mr. Harris will show the purport.

' One only thing has been a terrible pang to me,' she writes, ' the giving over of my own judgment in questions of moral judgment to any human authority. It is so absolutely new and incomprehensible an idea to me that any outer test should supplant, without risk to itself and me, the inner test of my actions that my conscience affords, that when . . . I decided to shut my eyes and leave the seeing to you I felt as though I were putting out the one clear light that had been given to me for my guidance . . . as though I had suddenly thrown my compass overboard and was left with my whole life exposed to the chances of a sea of uncertainty, and with the grim question asking itself over and over again in my heart, whether I were not doing wrong ? I answered myself, at first more mechanically than with any conviction, that anyhow one thing in me was

assuredly wrong, the want of humility that added the
sting to the anxiety, and that, in some way I could not
quite yet understand, the only thing by which I could
break this pride in pieces must end in being right.
So I am dealing to the best of my present powers with
this mischief. . . . And I tell you of it, that you may
learn all I can find to say of the weakness and faults
that will want what help you will give them, and not
because you shall never find in me any but the most
absolute submission both in deed and will. I hope and
believe I shall have bruised even this inward resistance
long before it could run the risk of throwing upon you
or anyone else any part of the suffering which ought to
belong only to me. So now I ask to put myself and ourselves under your direction in all matters. You will
determine what proof we must acquire to ourselves
that we hold our happiness in absolute fief to our duty ;
in what manner, when you think it well, we shall inaugurate the joining of our lives ; and the degree in
which we can usefully comply with or disregard the
prejudices of my family and friends on the subject of
performing the marriage ceremony, and disposing of
the property belonging to me.'

Thus, in all seriousness and sincerity Alice yielded
her will and bowed before the prophet she had never
seen, and at last the desired permission came. There
was trouble, indeed, on her side of the family, as her
letter showed. But Laurence and his bride had no
fears. They and all they had were at the disposal of the
prophet, for he alone could lead them on the way of

salvation. Laurence and Alice were married in London in 1872, and for a year they were allowed to live happily in Paris ; then, as suddenly as before the call came to return to Brocton, and Laurence and his wife and mother obeyed it at once. New orders awaited them ; ' Father ' instantly separated husband and wife, and set Alice to the task of ' putting off the old and much admired refinement, polish and intellectual charm,' and learning in its place how to attend to the house and rear chickens. While she was undergoing this probation, Laurence was sent out into the world again to conduct a number of financial enterprises from which Harris hoped for wealth. Lady Oliphant stayed at Brocton, still washing handkerchiefs, still separated from her son, but a little comforted by the presence of his wife.

Year after year this curious arrangement lasted. Laurence travelled to and fro, and went several times alone to England, still writing articles, and still working faithfully for the good of the whole community.

Meanwhile, at Brocton, Harris made the discovery that Alice was not her husband's counterpart. In 1876 he bought a property at Santa Rosa, in California, and moved the most fully initiated of his disciples there ; and Alice, but not Lady Oliphant, was of the number. Two years later Laurence followed them, apparently without permission, hoping for a sight of his wife ; but he was refused admittance, and although he waited about for several weeks, he finally accepted his rejection, and returned to Brocton, still obedient, though very much cast down by the stern decree.

Very soon after this Harris discovered in Alice strong resemblances to his own counterpart, Lily Queen ; and whether from this or some other unknown cause, she made a sudden departure from Santa Rosa. Still, however, the prohibition against joining Laurence was in force, and still she believed in the authority of 'Father'. She betook herself alone to an outpost town, and earned her living by teaching.

Laurence meanwhile went on with his devoted service, and once more went to London alone in 1879 ; there he threw himself into a scheme for the colonisation of Palestine, which led him to travel there and in Turkey, hoping for a concession from the Sultan. The whole thing failed, and in 1880 he was in London again, and there, suddenly, his wife at last joined him. Whether she was a little disillusioned with Harris is not clear ; but certainly the bond still held to some extent, and the allegiance was not broken off. The next year Laurence himself went back alone to Brocton to see his mother, who was still washing handkerchiefs there. He found her ill in body and troubled in mind. Rumours of Harris's peculiar way of life at Santa Rosa were disturbing the Brocton group, from which the master had now been absent over five years, and Lady Oliphant was very anxious to know the truth. She was, however, seriously ill, though Laurence refused to believe it, feeling convinced that she was in such perfect communion with her counterpart, his father, that heavenly strength was sustaining her. He took her trouble of mind much more seriously, and together they went to California to seek an explanation of the evil reports from Harris himself. They still hoped that all could be put right, and that the prophet they had been blindly obeying for so many years would re-establish his hold over their doubting hearts. When they reached him at last, however, they met with a very cold reception. Instead of explanations, reproaches and rebukes were heaped upon their heads, and they were bidden to be gone. And everything they saw and heard confirmed their worst fears. In great trouble and distress they moved on towards a 'cure' of which they had some hopes, but on the way there Lady Oliphant grew worse, and died in great suffering, believing to the very last that she was perfectly safe. With this blow the scales fell from Laurence's eyes. He was reduced to misery and distress and physical illness, but his allegiance to Harris had melted away and he even authorized some of his friends to begin a lawsuit for the recovery of some of the property which had been made over to 'Father'. From that moment there was war between the disciple and the master.

Alice, meanwhile, was in England, as yet faithful ; and it was Harris himself who opened her eyes. He, hoping to score a victory in the legal battle which was waging between the two men, took steps to have Laurence certified as insane. To complete this business, of course, the consent of his relatives was needed, and Harris cabled to Alice peremptorily ordering her to send this consent. The effect was the opposite of what he had intended. Alice's eyes too were opened, and when

Laurence was at length well enough to rejoin her in 1882 they were of one mind, and the despotic rule which had hitherto governed their lives was over.

Although the scales had fallen from Laurence's and Alice's eyes in regard to Harris, the hold of the strange religion stood firm. Laurence Oliphant and his wife believed as ardently in counterparts as they did before ; they still thought the world would be transformed and mankind saved by this revelation, and they still meant to devote their whole lives to the spreading of this truth. They settled at Haifa, and established there not exactly a community, but a centre for the religion they were preaching. A certain number of believers corresponded with them, and visited them, and they wrote together the strange book ' Sympneumata ', in which their faith is set forth even more obscurely than in any of the writings of Thomas Lake Harris. There too Laurence wrote his incredible novel, ' Masollam ', in which he gave a picture of Harris as unmistakable as it is bewildering. The hidden forces over which they believed he had had control remained at their command; the great truths which he had perverted were theirs to preach. For Laurence himself said they ' tried to push the world on a little further by placing two or three young couples, who were not married, in a tempting proximity in order to teach them the habit of self control ' ; and, in this extraordinary fashion they began to spread the light.

Alice Oliphant died in January, 1886, and Laurence was prostrated by the loss. In spite of his honest belief that she was with him still as his heavenly counterpart, he mourned for her bitterly ; and the fact that in less than two years he was married again was but a proof of his bereavement. For her spirit, or some other guiding, led him to return to America, and inspired him to seek the acquaintance of Rosamond Dale Owen, a leading Spiritualist. In her he immediately recognised something which he felt to be a part of his lost Alice, and they were married at once. He told his friends that his position as a teacher of hidden truths was difficult, especially as he must of necessity talk much of the relations of the sexes, and of the importance of female influence. His special leading to attract women disciples increased his troubles, and it was hardly possible for him to pursue his mission without a wife. This argument, and the obvious sincerity of his mourning for Alice, satisfied his friends and comforted his admirers ; but scandal was more difficult to avoid than he supposed. There were two young people, a brother and a sister, whom he had converted to his views, who were anxious to join him at Haifa and to make over the whole of their fortune for the propagation of the doctrine. Their friends became exceedingly alarmed, not only by the financial side of the affair, but also by rumours of the nature of Oliphant's teaching, and in desperation they lodged a complaint with the National Vigilance Association. An action in the courts for ' detournement de mineurs ' was pending in 1888 when Laurence fell desperately ill and died ; and the public revelations which would have been inevitable were never made.

Harris, all this time, had been preaching and practising the old doctrine. The defection of the Oliphants had been a severe blow, and had caused much bitterness and ill-feeling. A great many diatribes went forth against the deserters, which however fell short of their mark, in spite of the fury which inspired them. One single example, out of hundreds, will be enough to show the nature of the attack.

'Here and there,' wrote Harris in the pamphlet, 'God's Breath in Man' (published in 1891), 'as the fact of a new respiration creeps into slow publicity, Nature, whose art is endless imitation, occasionally frolics in men and women of conceited thought and mediumistic temperament for a simulated breath-play. These counterfeits are however easily detected ; first of all by the pompous arrogance of their assumptions, and by the vanity and egoism of their lives. If the note of danger is to be sounded it must be at the ensuing. There are also magical respirations both simple and complex, resultant from the practice of hypnotic arts, from efforts for self-penetration among experimenters in occult sciences, and from mediumistic initiations among spiritualists, from possessions and obsessions, and also from the intrusion of larvous and ghostly effigies into the structures of mental and passional sensation. . . .'

Whether it was the intrusion of 'larvous and ghostly effigies' or merely the result of the law-suit by which Oliphant sought to recover his property, the Community at Brocton came to an end, and such of the faithful as

had no ' conceited thought ' or ' mediumistic temperament ' congregated at Santa Rosa. The family there
was small, but it was exceedingly strange ; and the time
came when scandals began to gather about it too. A
lady who was anxious to join the Brotherhood came to
lodge near by, and as she saw it closer, her desire to
become a disciple vanished. She told such tales, and
spread such shocking stories of the household that the
interest of the neighbourhood became aroused. Harris
still maintained that ' angels were at work changing
the chosen ones into the arch-natural state ready for the
Second Coming. They clean out the inside ', he declared,
' and leave only a husk of humanity, and unload all the
grosser parts upon the damned '. It was no good.
Temporally minded people refused to admit the ' universal scope and purity ' of the doings of the ' cleaned-out
husks ', and in 1901 Harris felt himself constrained by the
force of public opinion to marry his leading disciple,
and leave the State. After that his influence ended.
He was an old man, and no longer a prophet. His
disciples were sadly disillusioned, and fell away ; and
with his death the whole dreadful business ended,
leaving only a warning and a black memory in the world
behind.

CHAPTER IX

LATER RELIGIOUS EXPERIMENTS; THE KORESHANS, AND THE HOUSE OF DAVID

ONEIDA and the Brotherhood of the New Life were experiments of the middle of the century, but the last fifty years of it saw other equally extraordinary phenomena, which, although they resemble their predecessors in many particulars, are worth mention if only to prove that the failure and collapse of one delusion is no safeguard against the uprising of another, equally pernicious and equally absurd.

In 1861 the little sect of Adonai Shomo (said to be the Hebrew words for The Lord, the Spirit is there) made its appearance in Massachusetts. Its leader, Frederick Howland, had first been a Quaker, then was converted by the Millerites, and finally in 1855 received the gift of tongues. Followed by a small band of believers who expected to attain to 'the Melchisedec Priesthood' he set up a small communistic society which lasted till 1896. Howland believed that death had lost its power over him and his followers, and although he was himself killed in a carriage accident in 1871 this faith survived. The leadership was taken over by a man named Cook, who claimed to be Christ's Viceregent, but who was in reality an ex-convict of vicious habits. No precise records of the developments of this venture remain, but there is an obituary notice in one of the histories of Communistic experiments from which the whole story may easily be deduced. ' Cook', the sentence runs, 'instituted such revolting practices as led to his indictment before a Grand Jury, and subsequent imprisonment'. And with this Adonai Shomo ended.

In 1876 a Revival in Texas led to a curious community, which, though it was never accused of ' revolting practices ' was sufficiently original to be worth describing. At the time it began, Mrs. Martha MacWhirter, its leader, was a married woman, living with her husband and twelve children in a small Southern town. She and some of her women friends began to study the Bible, as a consequence of a Revival which had come their way, and their study of the Holy Book led them to separate from the local Methodist Church to which they all belonged. A great commotion arose in the town, and when the 'Sanctified Band', as they called themselves, refused to send their children to Sunday School, and insisted on teaching them at home, and moreover on teaching them that the formalities of the Church were wicked, the commotion increased. The husbands of these intrepid ladies were chased through the streets and beaten, their houses were stoned, and the civic authorities issued a decree (which however was never enforced), that they must all leave the town. Great was the tribulation in the MacWhirter family. Nothing could shake Martha, nothing could make her yield ; and her poor husband with much regret joined the general wife-deserting movement which followed.

The Sanctified Band were undismayed. It is true that their economic position was desperate—since they had hitherto been supported by their husbands, and were now left without means ; but they were sure that the Lord would provide. They stuck together, eighteen in number, and divided up the little money they had. They then set to work to earn what they could, one taking in washing, one going out to daily service, one cutting timber, and one opening a boarding house. By rigid economy and ceaseless industry they kept alive, and before very long they were considerably more prosperous than they had been in the old days before their husbands left them. The boarding house developed into a hotel, and other hotels were added to it, and by 1898 they were such substantial citizens that one of them, though a woman, was elected to the local Board of Trade. By this time they had abandoned the name of the Sanctified Band, and were known as the ' Woman's Commonwealth ', and presently they decided to move to Washington. Their city, which had once tried to expel them, now begged and implored them to remain, but to no purpose. To the capital they went, and there continued to flourish, surviving even the death of the founder in 1904, and holding firmly to their celibacy, their community of goods, and their protest against outward forms. Although in name they were a female movement, they always declared that men were free to join them, and did actually have some male members at one time ; but only one of these men could endure the atmosphere of the group for long, and even he finally departed.

144

The Lord's Farm, which was founded by P. B. Mnason in 1877, a year after the Woman's Commonwealth, was similar in its main ideas. Celibacy, and the rejection of outward forms, combined with a strict following of the precepts of the Bible (as Mnason understood them) was the basis of the creed, but with these people community of goods was carried to a further extreme. Not only did they share what they had with each other, but with everyone who came their way. The doors of their ' City of God ' (which they sometimes called The Lord's Farm, and sometimes the Land of Rest and Peace, and sometimes the State of Eternal Bliss) stood open to every comer, and tramps and vagrants gathered there year after year. The community was, however, sufficiently vigorous to withstand this infliction, and lived and nourished itself on fruit, vegetables and fanatical words for many years. In 1890 this community was under the leadership of H. T. Mnason, presumably a son of its founder. It still carried on the same line of conduct, but had substituted free love for celibacy, and added a frenzied dancing to its previous absence of ritual. Under this regime the community was given the name of 'Angel Dancers', and its meetings, which were held in the open air, were visited by many sightseers. After grace was said before meals, the true believers were accustomed to leap over the table, in proof that the devil was vanquished, and they were at all times on the look out for his arrival. The custom of welcoming all comers was continued, and so many bad characters collected at the Lord's Farm that the civil authorities intervened, and in 1893 sent Mnason and some of his companions to prison for 'malicious mischief, and maintaining a disorderly house'. The believers took their persecution in good part, and went on with their community when they were liberated, remaining to the end honest and successful farmers, whom it was impossible to rouse to anger, or to persuade that any of their visitors were rogues. In time, however, the adherents died off, and there were said to be only twelve of them in 1908.

Mrs. Beckman, of the Church Triumphant, gathered her followers to the number of three or four hundred in Illinois in 1880. Her claim was that she was the mother—or at any rate the spiritual mother—of Christ in His Second Incarnation. The course of her triumph ran more or less smoothly until the Christ was made known ; but when her disciples learnt that he was a young German named G. J. Schweinfurth there was doubt and division in the camp. The young man himself was a simple and harmless youth, who lived mainly in a cave, and did not cut his beard ; but Mrs. Beckman's claims were disputed, a party arose which objected to female leadership, and in the usual fashion this sect, like all the others, disappeared.

The Koreshans, who began in 1870 were less transitory. Their prophet, Cyrus R. Teed, was born in 1839, and 'illuminated' when he was about thirty years old. His illumination had many points in common with St. Simonism, though there is no evidence that he was aware of the fact. Like Enfantin and Bazard he believed that the world was to be ruled by a man and a woman together, of whom the woman was to be the greater ; but, unlike his unhappy predecessors, he found the woman and his ' central duality ' was complete.

The Koreshans believed in an elaborate ' Cellular Cosmogony', and followed a ritual which they thought was modelled upon the motions of the stars and planets. Their New Jerusalem, ' the vitellus of the Cosmogenic Egg ' was situated at Estero, Florida, but they had one or two smaller establishments, and the total of their resident members was about five hundred, and they claimed in addition ten thousand adherents in the world outside. Korishanty, they thought, would super-sede Christianity, as Christianity had superseded Judaism, and in the meantime they organised the ' Society of the Arch-Triumphant ' in several American cities. Their settlement was however their chief effort, and there they practised community life combined with vegetarianism and frequent religious ceremonies. They allowed marriage in a modified form, but preferred celibacy ; and they claimed that part of their mission was to reconcile all the races of the world.

All this is familiar doctrine, and had frequently been believed before the Koreshans appeared upon the scene. But the long rigmarole of their creed contained one thing which was both novel and comprehensible, and which marks it out from among the other sects in a somewhat astonishing way. This article of faith taught that the woman leader of the Community, Victoria Gratia as she was called, would one day execute the man leader, Cyrus R. Teed (Koresh), after which her greatest work would begin ! Teed himself spoke freely to visitors of this coming event, and confessed that he did not know the time nor the manner of his impending murder, but that when it was accomplished he was sure ' the chosen woman of the age will be exalted into divine motherhood and imperial pre-eminence as the divine-natural head of all orders of Church and State.'

It is curious to speculate upon the feelings and intentions of Victoria Gratia during the long years while this crime was impending. Her portrait shows her to be a tall large woman, with dark hair elaborately waved, and a wide mouth. There are no signs of her dreadful mission in her face which though it seems hard and arrogant has no tragic expression ; and in the event the mission failed. Cyrus R. Teed died a natural death, and Koreshanty has as yet shown no sign of replacing Christianity.

The House of David is the last of the communities to be considered. Its downfall is of recent occurrence, and the revelations with which it was accompanied have shocked the whole country, and given a widespread warning against the follies and evils of religious extravagance. The reason for including an account of this community here is not so much to add to an already forcible warning as to show how close was its relation to the other sects and how far from original or isolated its peculiarities were.

Benjamin Purnell, and Mary his wife, who were

jointly the Shiloh, or seventh Messenger of the last dispensation, were natives of the State of Kentucky, and their first religious experience was with a short lived colony of Southcottians in Detroit, whose leader, Michæl Mills, was sent to prison for the ill-treatment of young girls.

After this, Benjamin and Mary set up for themselves and in 1907 the centre of the sect was at Benton Harbour, Michigan, where there was a settlement of over seven hundred people, and where preparations were being made for the 144,000 men and 144,000 women whom they believed to be the children of Israel, now scattered like lost sheep among the Gentiles, but destined to be saved on the Last Day. They claimed to possess the same revelation as had been vouchsafed to Joanna Southcott, which had been passed on through John Wroe and James Jezreel, and four other intermediaries to Mary and David themselves.

Their beliefs included the familiar delusion that they were exempt from mortal death, and the revelation that for the Gentiles the end of the world was due in August, 1916. They preached and practised community of goods, even extending it to wearing apparel, and they preached (if they did not practise) entire chastity. They wore simple clothes, and the men did not cut or shave their hair ; they spent much of their time in music, for which purpose they maintained several brass bands and an orchestra, and they carried on an extensive publishing business, for the diffusion of their own works. They had a monthly paper, ' The

Flying Roll ', which set forth their ideas amid a mass of flamboyant verbiage, and their four sacred ' Books of Wisdom ' propounded the Three Glories : the Origin of Evil, True Circumcision, and the Coming of Shiloh to their own entire satisfaction, and to the bewilderment of the Gentile mind.

All went well, and much money came into the community, but in 1923 troubles arose. A family of believers suddenly lost their faith, and brought a civil and criminal action against King Benjamin and his associates for appropriating £40,000, and for assaulting two young girls, driving another insane, and generally conducting the community in an immoral and unlawful manner. During the course of the preliminary hearing before the Grand Jury, Benjamin disappeared, and when the police came to arrest him he was nowhere to be found. Large rewards were offered, and he was sought for all over the world, but it was not until the end of 1926 that the police got a hint of his whereabouts from two disillusioned members. Then followed a dramatic scene. A body of mounted police armed with axes and searchlights entered the community grounds in the middle of the night and broke into Shiloh, the central building, where in a luxurious secret underground room the prophet was found. The revelations which followed closed the history of the House of David and the career of its King.

With this final example the list of religious and communistic failures must end. There were indeed many more in the latter half of the nineteenth century which are not chronicled here, and there are many still in existence which began at that time. But contemporary attempts to reform the world are not carried on in quite the same atmosphere as the earlier adventures. The blaze of publicity which now attends any unusual enterprise, and the limelight of journalistic exaggeration which accompanies it have swept away the innocent unsophisticated public to which such creeds used to appeal. Modern prophets and evangelists get their followers by a different method. They have their business and publicity managers, their advertisement agents and their official photographers. Their creeds may be as dangerous and as perverted as those of their predecessors, but the atmosphere in which they exist has changed. And this book is an attempt to show the conditions amid which Hannah Whitall Smith's personal experiences of fanaticism were acquired. She made her explorations into this strange world between the years 1850 and 1880, and moved among people who had seen in their youth the rise of the Fourierite Movement, and who had lived through the Civil War. After 1880, though her interest in these marvels still continued, her faith in their possibly divine origin was gone. She watched the newspapers for accounts of new sects, and preserved a mass of documents recording their downfall ; but was herself content to leave them alone.

Among the papers she collected there are many queer tales of false Christs and false Moseses; there are descriptions of orgies of religious excitement, and accounts of impending Days of Judgment. There is the story of Sandford, who set out singlehanded to build a vast temple to the Lord, and who built it. There is the story of Dowie, and the multitude he led forth to the New Zion, with a brightly coloured map of that peculiar city. There is the awful tale of the man who took his son up on to a mountain, offering him, as Abraham offered Isaac to the Lord, which tells how, since this hand was not stayed, he killed the boy. There is an account of the bonfire movement, when excited people threw into the flames all that they held most precious on earth, until at last a woman threw in her infant child, hoping thus to please the Lord. All these and a hundred more examples of the limitless folly of mankind are recorded in her collection, and are to be found in the newspapers of the end of the century. But since she knew them only at second-hand, and since they have already been so fully and so publicly recorded, they can be omitted. It is enough to know in detail the delusions of one single age.

The forces of diseased imagination are playing still upon the mass of the ill-educated and ignorant, bringing disaster and pitiful human tragedy in their train. Though they take different forms to-day, miracles, marvels, false hopes and vain delusions are still betraying men's emotions and confounding their senses, and disaster still comes into the world from the false promptings of the spirit. Subconscious impulses still disguise themselves as inspiration, and mankind still seeks Divine sanction for its secret, uncomprehended desires. For Babylon is not fallen, and ' the smoke of their torment ascendeth up for ever and ever '.

PERSONAL EXPERIENCES OF
FANATICISM

BY

HANNAH WHITALL SMITH

CHAPTER I

EXPLANATION OF FANATICISM

A FTER careful study of the subject of Fanaticism, and a great deal of most intimate intercourse with the Fanatics, I have come to the conclusion that the whole explanation of it lies in the fact that the emotional nature is allowed absolute control. The subject of the emotional nature is one of the mysteries that have never yet been fully solved ; but one thing is very certain : it is the most uncontrollable part of our nature, and the least to be depended upon. Everything affects our emotional nature : the state of one's health, the state of the weather, the sort of food we eat, the atmosphere we live in, the circumstances of our lives, whether pleasant or otherwise, and especially, and more than anything else, the influence of other people upon us. Emotions are more contagious than the most contagious disease in the universe. We all know that if we see one person yawn we are more than likely to do it ourselves, and if one person cries in a company it is very apt to set the whole company crying. I have noticed this with regard to deaths : you can bear the death of someone you love with quiet resignation when alone, but if you meet a person who begins to cry about it, off you go at once and cry about it yourself, not because the trial is any worse, but because you have caught the contagion of emotion. It is the same way with laughing ; and, in fact, with almost every feeling. A cheerful person can cheer up a whole circle of unhappy people, and a depressed person can depress the most cheerful, and all this often without a word being said, but simply by the mysterious, contagious power of emotion. In the whole history of religion this has been very marked. In all the strange manifestations of the Middle Ages, when whole communities would dance, or would flagellate themselves, or would fall into trances, or do all sorts of strange and fanatical things, the whole thing can be traced entirely to the contagion of emotion. And in these modern fanaticisms which I shall describe, this element of emotional contagion was always most marked. Of course the special and strongest emotions of our nature are the emotions of our affections and our passions, and invariably in every fanaticism that I have known the emotion of passion has sooner or later been aroused and given predominance. Among the old Mystics there can be found the diagram of a religious thermometer marked in its different degrees with the emotions likely to be produced, and among these, very prominently, is marked the emotion of passion. As far as I have known it, no fanatic ever began with the least idea of this, but they have been led on to it by slow and imperceptible degrees, and landed in the final issue before they knew where they were. The first beginning of this emotional evolution comes generally from the fact that people take their inward impressions as being the voice of the Lord. I cannot speak too strongly about this. Every fanaticism that I have ever known has begun by the following of these inward impressions. It is a most delightful doctrine to believe that God guides His people, and that it is really true that 'the steps of a good man are ordered by the Lord', and it is very natural that every Christian heart should want to know this guidance. The difficulty is how to get at it, and one of the easiest solutions of this difficulty seems very often to lie in a yielding to interior impressions. We know that the voice of the Lord is supposed to be an interior voice and that therefore it can only be heard within the soul. When people are in specially religious frames of mind, their emotional nature is always specially open to impressions, and it is certainly the most natural thing in the world for them to believe that the interior impressions which come in these solemn and sacred moments must necessarily be of the Lord. I cannot tell how many fanatics, when I have tried to convince them of their errors, have said to me : ' But, Mrs. Smith, what *am* I to do ? These inward voices come to me in my most solemn and sacred moments, when I feel myself to be nearest the Lord and most abandoned to Him, and how can I believe that at such moments He would allow the delusions of the devil to deceive me ? ' The mistake arises from limiting the voice of the Lord to impressions only, and not recognizing that His voice comes to us in many other ways, and that the real voice of the Lord must be one in which all His different voices harmonize. For, as I have shown in my chapter on Guidance, God speaks to us in many different voices, and no one voice, however powerful or impressive it may be, must be taken as authoritative unless it is in harmony with God's other voices on the same subject. It stands to reason that God cannot tell us a thing in one voice and tell us exactly the opposite in another. If He says, for instance, in the Bible, 'Thou shalt not steal', He cannot possibly say in the voice of an inward impression, 'Thou must steal'. His voices may be many, but His message can be but one. If there is a contradiction in the voices, the speaker cannot be the same.

Therefore, in giving themselves up to the guidance of the voice of interior impressions only, without regard to the other voices by which God speaks, Christians enter upon a pathway of the utmost danger. Nothing is more unreliable than these interior impressions taken alone, and, what is worse, nothing is more contagious.

When an earnest Christian, who is seeking to know the guidance of the Lord, hears of another Christian being guided in a certain direction, it is ten to one that he will have the same guidance. I do not consider this to be specially of the devil, but simply and only a fact of human nature which has never been half enough realized or understood. Therefore, if you are in a company of people who profess to know the voice of the Lord, it is most unsafe to yield yourself to their influence without bringing in the balancing power of God's other voices of which I have spoken ; and the only real safe guidance ever to follow is one's conviction of right. These convictions are always made up of the harmony of God's four especial voices, i.e. the voice of the Bible, the voice of circumstances, the voice of one's highest reason, and the voice of one's inward impressions. Of course, one's interpretation of these various voices will necessarily be in accordance with the standard of right and wrong which surrounds one. For instance, I can imagine a religious and ignorant person interpreting God's voices to mean something which might be entirely right in his own circle, but which would be entirely wrong in a circle more enlightened than his own. The time has not yet arrived in the history of the human race when in this world we can have any absolute standard of right and wrong, for even in following the Lord Jesus Christ we are each one biased by the way we look upon what He did, and the explanations we give to His teaching. We must therefore believe in each other's honesty of purpose as much as we believe in our own, and we must grant that what may seem wrong to us may seem right to another person whose outlook is on a different plane from our own.

To go back to the way in which fanaticism grows : Christians begin with an earnest desire to know entire consecration to the Lord in a faithful following of Him whithersoever He shall lead. They take their inward impressions as being the only voice in which God communicates with them, and feel that loyalty requires that they shall follow these impressions without regard to any other consideration. I have known the dearest and sweetest saints in the world started on a career of fanaticism by simply taking the ground that, when things looked strange or doubtful they must, as they express it, give the Lord the benefit of the doubt : that is, if they are not quite sure whether a thing is right or wrong they must judge by whether it is hard or easy : if it is hard, then they must believe it is of the Lord and must do it : if it is easy, then they must believe it is of the devil and not do it. This to my mind is an utterly mistaken foundation. I believe that we never ought to act in doubt, but ought always to wait for an inward conviction that the thing really is right or wrong. Our Lord Himself said that His sheep should know His voice, not be in doubt about it, but be sure of it, and unless a sheep is sure of his shepherd's voice it is a fatal mistake for it to follow. Positive certainty must be the necessary foundation of all God's guidance, and this certainty can only be arrived at by the harmony of every voice in which He speaks. Embryo fanatics, however, know nothing of this, and believe that they are most faithful and obedient when they follow every impression that they receive. Naturally the impressions, being encouraged in this way, grow in power, and as the emotional nature is thus aroused more and more, it is a very simple matter for that part of the nature which is most emotional to be in course of time aroused also. It generally begins with physical thrills, which in themselves are a perfectly natural manifestation of the emotional nature, and which only become dangerous when they are looked upon, yielded to and encouraged as being of divine origin. All human beings know about these thrills. We are very apt to feel them at the sight of some deed of heroism, or the hearing of the story of it, or the sight of some beautiful picture, or the hearing of an eloquent speech, or the reception of some stirring piece of news ; in short, on the occasion of any circumstance, whether religious or otherwise, which is calculated to arouse the emotional nature. These thrills proceed, no doubt, from that part of our nervous system in which passion resides : they are, as I said, perfectly natural and contain no cause for alarm, but when yielded to and indulged in they do become harmful : and, sooner or later, they lead to the development of the passional nature to such an extent as to become perfectly uncontrollable. In the case of fanatics these thrills are very apt to accompany the discovery of new truth, or the quickening of the affections in devotion to the Lord ; they are the natural physical accompaniments of the awakened spiritual nature. In emotional people they are much stronger, naturally, than in calmer, quieter people, and are more likely to gain absolute control. The whole mistake lies in attributing these physical sensations to a divine origin ; they are no more divine in the religious life than they are when seeing a fine picture, or hearing fine music. I have heard many people say with regard to Wagner's music that it went through them with thrills of delight, and yet nobody attributes these thrills to God. They are not a divine touch in the case of music, and they are not a divine touch in the case of religion ; they are simply the physical response to the spiritual frame of mind, whatever may cause it. But one can see that it would be very natural for Christians who have had this physical response in their own bodies to some wonderful spiritual truth, to think that these physical thrills are the divine touch and the token of the divine presence, and that therefore they ought to be sought after and cultivated with all possible earnestness, especially as they may never have felt them at any other time. Moreover, as they really are very delightful, it is a temptation to cultivate such delightful feelings and to give oneself up to them.

I knew one dear lady who began in the purest and simplest way to give herself up to these emotions, and gradually came to spending most of her time allowing these waves of thrills to flow through her from head to foot, believing that she was in this way realizing more and more the presence of the Lord, and coming more and more into actual union with Him. And the result was most disastrous in destroying her moral nature, and launching her into a course of impurity from which in the beginning she would have shrunk with horror. In the case of every fanatic I have known this has been the process, and sooner or later, unless some rather unusual amount of good common sense comes in to deliver the soul, it must end in a sort of physical debauchery which will either make inward or outward havoc of the life. It is of no use to talk to people under these circumstances. Their emotions are too powerful to be checked by argument ; you might as well hope to check Niagara by argument. The only hope is that Christians may be so warned in the beginning, as to be able to see the danger that lies before them, and therefore avoid it.

The fanaticisms of Thomas Harris, and of his follower, Laurence Oliphant, followed exactly the course I have here sketched, beginning in an honest and earnest desire to follow the Lord whithersoever He might lead, and ending in the most flagrant and open immorality. It was the same with the doctor of the New York Sanatorium where those strange secrets of union with Christ were explained to me. Never was there a saintlier man to begin with, and never was there a more pitiful fall. In fact, this has been the course of every fanaticism I have known about. Sooner or later Christians, who give themselves up to follow impressions, become the slaves of their emotional natures, and end in giving to their carnal passions the place of authority they have meant to give to God. I have watched my own experiences in these respects very carefully, and compared them with those of a very intimate friend of mine whose nature was far more emotional than my own. We were seekers together after the deep things of God, and whenever I made what I thought was a discovery of a new truth I always at once confided it to her. And I found that, while in my own case the discovery had been only a keen intellectual delight, in her case it nearly always caused an awakening of her emotions, accompanied very frequently with wave after wave of delicious physical thrills. She always called these thrills the 'witness of the Spirit' to the truth we had discovered, and, until I had a clearer understanding of the subject, I often felt greatly disappointed that I seemed debarred from receiving this longed-for 'witness'. But I discovered at last that the differences in our experiences came entirely from the differences in the susceptibilities of our emotional natures, her emotions always responding in physical sensations where my emotions responded in intellectual convictions. I discovered further that my convictions were far more permanent than her emotions, and that the truths we had discovered simultaneously remained an actual power in my life long after the impressions on her emotions had passed away and left nothing behind them, and I became at last very sceptical of any religious life founded upon the emotions, and realised that conviction was the only safe foundation.

I would, therefore, always urge every seeker after the deep things of God to ignore emotions and care only for convictions. If emotions come one may enjoy them for what they are worth, and I acknowledge that they are often very enjoyable ; but one must never in the least depend upon them, but must be satisfied with nothing short of actual and downright convictions. And I would place at the entrance into the pathway of mysticism this danger signal : Beware of impressions, beware of emotions, beware of physical thrills, beware of voices, beware of everything, in short, that is not according to the strict Bible standard and to your own highest reason.

With this preface I will now relate some of my explorations into the region of fanaticism, beginning with my first introduction to it.

CHAPTER II

DR. R.'S FANATICISM

ONE of the most mysterious phases of the religious life is the phase of fanaticism. As it has happened to me to come into close and intimate contact with many of the leading delusions which are apt to mislead Christians, and as I know that people fall into them mostly because of ignorance, I feel that I ought to tell my experiences in order to warn those who may be tempted into similar pathways. I must say first of all that all the fanatics I have ever known have been at the same time the most devoted of Christians, and have fallen into their fanaticisms along the paths of the most entire consecration to the Lord, and the most absolute faith in His guidance. And all my own intercourse with them was always because I myself was seeking to know all that could be known of the 'life hid with Christ in God', and was hungering and thirsting after an expression of entire consecration and perfect trust. That I was not led completely astray in this search arose not from any extra piety on my part, for as a general thing I was not so pious really as the dear fanatics themselves, but because of two facts, one fact being that I am not of an emotional nature, and have always had to receive religious truth through my intellect rather than through my emotions, and the other fact being that at the bottom

I have a sort of weight of common sense which, like those weighted toy-men which amuse children by always turning head up no matter how much they may be tumbled over, seemed generally to turn me right side up no matter how far over I might be pushed. But I had also a very mystical side to my nature which longed for direct revelations from God and for manifest tokens of His presence, and for many years I sought in every direction to find a satisfaction for this craving. I never heard of anyone having a 'remarkable experience', or a 'wonderful revelation' that I did not rush off at once to know all about it, and to find out how I could get the same. And fanatics of every sort and description found in me the most sympathetic and appreciative listener, and the most humble and eager scholar. As what I wanted was to *get at the core* of what they had to tell, and to find out if possible the real thing at the bottom of all their delusions and vagaries, I never allowed myself to be shocked at anything they might say, but gave them genuine sympathy, even where I could not approve, and in consequence a great deal more was poured out to me than ordinarily would have been the case, and hence it is that I came to know about and am able to give the inside history of so much fanaticism.

The beginning of it all was in the year 1871 or '72, when my husband needed a course of treatment for a nervous breakdown. We took our family to a Hydropathic Sanatorium in New York State, and we stayed there for three or four months. The head of the establishment was one of the most saintly men I ever met. No one could be in his presence without feeling that he was a man who lived in continual nearness and communion with the Lord. It was not that he talked so much about religion, but it seemed to be in his looks, his atmosphere, his actions, and in everything about him. A very dear friend of mine was staying in the Sanatorium at the same time ; and as we were both hungering and thirsting to know the deep things of God, we very often had long conversations about it. One day she said to me, ' Hannah, I believe that Doctor R. knows some secrets of the divine life that thee and I ought to know : he has hinted as much to me when he has been seeing me about my health. Wouldn't thee like to have him tell us ? ' Of course I agreed to this with all my heart, and she decided to ask him. When I next saw her she said she had asked him, and he had told her that he would ask the Lord whether he was to reveal the secret to us or not. A few days later he told my friend that he had received permission from the Lord to tell us the secret, and he fixed a time when we were to meet to hear it. Naturally we were in a state of great excitement and prayed a great deal that we might be rightly guided in regard to it. Never shall I forget that interview. He began by telling us that the Baptism of the Holy Spirit was a physical thing, felt by delightful thrills going through you from head to foot, and that no one could really know what the Baptism of the Spirit was who did not experience these thrills. He said that this had been revealed to him in the following manner. He had been praying the Lord to give him the Baptism of the Holy Spirit, and he found that whenever he prayed especially earnestly he had physical thrills which he thought belonged to earthly passions. He blamed himself exceedingly for this, and thought what a sensual man he must be that in his most sacred moments such feelings should come. By fasting and prayer he would get deliverance, as he thought, and would then begin to pray again for the Baptism of the Holy Spirit, but invariably, after a short time of prayer, the sensations would return, and the same process of fasting and prayer would have to be gone through. As this happened over and over he was at last almost in despair. One day, however, when, during an earnest season of prayer, these sensations were particularly strong, an inward voice seemed to say, ' These sensations which you so much condemn are really the divine touch of the Holy Spirit in your body.' He said it was very hard for him to believe this, but it seemed to come with such divine authority that he dared not reject it. He asked specially for a sign that if it really were that Baptism of the Spirit for which he had been praying it might be made so plain to him that there could be no mistake. And this prayer, he said, had been unmistakably answered, and he had been convinced beyond a shadow of doubt that these very sensations, which he had condemned as being of the flesh, were actually the very Baptism of Spirit that he had longed for. Immediately, he said, he began to receive them with thankfulness, and the result was that they had become so continuous that there was hardly a moment in his life without them, and that he had found the greatest spiritual enlightenment and uplifting from the moment that he allowed himself to receive these sensations as being the touch of the Lord. This he told us was the divine secret which had been revealed to him, and which he was permitted to tell chosen souls. He urged us to take the subject before the Lord in prayer, and to ask Him to enlighten us, and he warned us not to let carnal thoughts concerning this blessed experience come in to blind our eyes to the divine realities it embodied. My friend and I had not dared to say a word while this revelation was being made to us, and when Dr. R. left we sat for a long while in dumbfounded silence. We were both utterly ignorant of the wiles of the devil in this direction, and we had such absolute confidence in the holiness of this saint of God, as he seemed to us, that we were afraid our horror at what he had told us must be because we were too carnally minded, as he had said, to be able to see the deep spiritual purity of it all, and we felt that we dared not reject it without further prayer and consideration. We had several further talks with Dr. R. about it, and he told us these 'baptisms' were really the fulfilment of the union between Christ and His people as the Bridegroom and the bride, described in Ephesians v, 23–32, and typified in the Song of Solomon, and declared in many parts of Scripture, and that to reject it was to reject union with the Lord Himself. And he described this spiritual union as being so enrapturing and uplifting, and so full of the Lord's actual presence, that at last we began to believe there must be something in it, and to long to know for ourselves the reality of this wonderful consecration. We could not accept *all* the details of the experience that Dr. R. gave us, but we did begin to believe that there was a physical ' touch ' of God, that manifested itself in a bewildering delicious sensation of a sort of magnetic thrill of divine life pouring through both soul and body, which lifted one up into an enrapturing realization of oneness with Christ and that this was the true 'Baptism of the Holy Ghost'. We came to the conclusion that it must be what all the old mystics had known, and that it was the true inner meaning of that Union with Christ for which saints of all ages had longed, and into the realization of which so many of them seemed to have entered. And we both began earnestly to seek to know it for ourselves. Before, however, any answer had come to our prayer my friend and I left the Sanatorium and were widely separated, and we have never met since. She, I believe, did at last come into something of the experience, but to me, in spite of all my prayers and searchings, it was always a sealed book. No spiritual experience I ever had, and I have had many delightful ones, ever affected me physically in the slightest degree, and although it was at first a great disappointment, I have long come to see, as I shall explain hereafter, that it was far best so. But at that time, and for many years, I hungered and thirsted for some tangible Baptism that would give me the enrapturing thrills of bliss others seemed to enjoy,

and would assure me that I really had received the
Baptism of the Holy Spirit for which my soul so eagerly
longed. And it was in the prosecution of this earnest
and prayerful search that I encountered the various forms
of fanaticism that I am about to describe.

I was always on the look out for anyone who had a
'wonderful spiritual experience,' and in each instance
fondly hoped, until my common sense asserted itself,
that now at last I had found the key that would open
to me the door of this mystic region of divine union.
As usual, when I was interested in anything, my friends
had to become interested too, and to all with whom
I dared to touch on such a sacred, yet delicate, subject,
I tried to tell what Dr. R. had told us. And in several
instances, both in England and America, those I told
of it received the baptism I described, and in each case
this very baptism was the opening up for them of a life
of union and communion with God far beyond anything
they had ever known before. Even to this day I continually meet with the lasting results in transformed
lives and in holy characters of Christians who had
entered into the experience. In many instances the
receiving of it by preachers was the beginning of great
revivals in their churches, and was, in fact, the initiation
of a great deal of the 'Holiness' movement of thirty
years ago. This movement took hold of the upper
classes, and the meetings were largely composed of
the aristocracy and the rich and influential people
in English Society. There was nothing sectarian in
the whole movement ; no one was asked, or in any way

influenced, to leave the Church to which they belonged. All that was desired was that people should act in daily life according to the doctrines they professed to believe. It was not so much a difference of belief as a difference of life, and one of the marvellous features of it was the union of people of all forms of belief, and of all denominational relationships without the least effort being made after this union. In looking back, I can see that this arose from the fact that we were dealing with the fundamental principle of all religion, namely, surrender to God and trust in Him. Dogmas and doctrines were of no account, and were never referred to, for they were not needed in the region in which this movement was carried on. It was the region of personal experience and absolute realities which must lie at the basis of every religion. If people worship God at all, they must necessarily have a great fund of common feeling upon which it is helpful to communicate with one another. But while great spiritual blessings have seemed often to be the result of this experience of union with God, very disastrous outward falls from purity and righteousness have sometimes followed, as will be seen in the following pages, and I have been convinced by all that I have seen and known that it is a dangerous path to enter upon and that it is of the utmost importance a danger signal should be erected at the entrance to it, in order that travellers thereon may be warned of the traps and pitfalls they are almost sure to meet.

CHAPTER III

MISS S.'S FANATICISM

ONE day, not long after our stay at that New York sanatorium, I was taking a walk when I noticed a young lady walking in front of me, whom I did not know, but whose *back* seemed to say to me that we were destined to become friends. Curiously enough, in a few minutes a friend of mine, coming towards us, stopped and spoke to this lady, and, when I caught up with them, introduced us to one another. The attraction appeared to be mutual, and we seemed after that to be continually thrown together. I found her a very interesting and talented person, very religious, and a most successful Christian worker, but rather self-absorbed. She was a very strict Friend, and dressed in the strictest fashion of sugar-scoop bonnets, crossed handkerchiefs, with a dainty three-cornered shawl over her shoulders. We became very intimate, and I was deeply interested in her religious life, and followed her various experiences with profound sympathy. She was very religious, and we soon discovered that we were both seekers after the mystic life, and especially after the baptism of the Holy Spirit, and we embraced every opportunity we could find of seeking for it together.

At that time some Methodists who believed in sanctification by faith were in the habit of holding in the summer what were called Holiness Camp Meetings.

These meetings were held at different places throughout the country during the warm American summers, in groves or forests, or on the borders of lakes, or by the seaside. They were generally held for ten days at a time, and were led by prominent religious preachers and teachers who believed in the doctrine of Holiness, or, in other words, of 'sanctification by faith'. Those who attended the meetings lived in tents dotted about under the trees, and for the whole ten days of the meeting all earthly cares and interests were as far as possible put aside, and the entire company gave themselves up to religious exercises and religious interests.

In the summer of 187— the friend of whom I speak and I myself, with a large company of congenial friends, attended one of these Camp Meetings, all of us hungering and thirsting after righteousness, and especially longing to know experimentally the conscious baptism of the Holy Spirit. The whole camp ground was exercised on this subject, and in almost every meeting wonderful testimonies would be given by those who had, as they believed, consciously received it.

Our expectations and our longings were wrought up to the highest pitch of enthusiasm, and one evening, after the public meeting under the trees was over, a few of us gathered in one tent for a special prayer meeting on the subject, determined to wrestle and agonise until the answer came. We knelt in the dark, and poured out our prayers and supplications, either aloud or in our own souls, literally 'with groanings that could not be uttered', for two or three hours. But to my great surprise no answer seemed to come, and at last, when the lateness of the hour compelled us to separate, it was with a feeling of unutterable disappointment on my part.

As the company passed out of the tent, I noticed my friend did not pass out with them, and I wondered whether she had slipped out silently before the meeting closed and gone back to her own tent. I lighted a candle to go to bed when, to my astonishment, I found her lying across the foot of my bed in what appeared to be a swoon. I spoke to her, and immediately she began to praise God in the most rapturous way : ' Oh, how wonderful ! Oh, how glorious ! Oh, this is the Baptism ! Oh, what a blessing ; 'tis more than I can bear ! Oh, Lord, stay Thy hand ! Flesh and blood cannot bear this glory ! ' And similar exclamations burst from her lips in tones of ecstacy. As may be imagined, I was overwhelmed with awe and delight, and I immediately rushed out to call in my friends to see the wonderful answer to our prayers, for I could not doubt that my friend had received that baptism of the Holy Spirit for which we were all longing. Why she had been picked out, I could not imagine, for she was not, as far as I knew, a bit better or a bit more earnest than any of the rest of us. However, there it was, and I determined to enjoy it at second-hand as much as ever I could.

A little awestruck company gathered round the bed, and eagerly drank in all her rapturous exclamations, afraid almost to breathe for fear we should disturb the heavenly visitation. After a while she seemed to recover from her swoon sufficiently to go to her own tent, and, although very tottering and scarcely able to walk, we managed to take her there and get her undressed and into bed. And then, determined not to lose a moment of this blissful visitation, I brought in my mattress and lay on the floor beside her bed so as to catch every word that fell from her lips, and also a little in hopes that some of the blessing might spill over on to me. The night was apparently a night of rapture to my friend, and early in the morning I sent word to the early Prayer Meeting of the great blessing that had come to the camp ground. Immediately a deputation of the leaders of the meeting came to the tent to ask my friend whether she would not come to their large meeting and bear testimony to the blessing that had been bestowed upon her. This request, however, seemed to shock her very much, as she said it would be like exposing one's dearest love-secrets to the public gaze, and she entirely refused to go, and blamed me very severely for having told of her experience and brought this exposure upon her. My own impression at the time was that her feeling of annoyance with me, and her refusal to testify, spoiled the blessing, for it very soon seemed to wane and she came back to ordinary life again. It was one of the foundation principles among believers in the definite baptism of the Holy Spirit that if you did not confess it when you had received it, it might be lost ; but I can understand now that she would naturally have been provoked with me for bringing in a company of comparative strangers to stand round her bed and listen to her raptures. Perhaps if I had stopped to think I should not have done it, but my mind was so set on the one thing, the Baptism of the Spirit, and so overwhelmed with delight at this apparently tangible answer to our prayers, that no other considerations entered into my head. Had it been myself, I should have wanted it proclaimed on the house-tops, as a definite sign of the presence and power of God. However, my friend was furious with me, and I cannot but believe that because of this she did lose whatever it was she had. But in spite of this it seemed to have been what the Swedenborgians call ' her opening into the spiritual world ', for, from that time she began to have very strange and wonderful experiences, which in the end became great fanaticisms. Having had such a blissful and rapturous time, she naturally found ordinary religious life very humdrum and uninteresting, and was continually reaching out for similar raptures. When I told her of my experiences at the water-cure, and of the secret that had there been revealed to me she immediately seized upon it as a probable opportunity for herself to regain her lost blessing, and went to this same water-cure, and put herself under the teaching of the doctor there, hoping that she also might learn his strange secrets. The result was that she went into the wildest extravagances. She embraced all his views, and felt led, as she fully believed by the Holy Spirit, to great lengths in the lines he taught. Among other things, she felt it her duty to ask him to stand naked before her, and also to do the same thing herself before him. To what other lengths she went I have never known, but she was fully imbued with the idea that the baptism of the Holy Spirit was physical as well as spiritual, and that the great aim of religious teachers should be to excite in themselves and in others those physical thrills which accompany passion, and which she had come to believe were the manifest token of union with Christ. She took the Song of Solomon to be the exposition of the relation between the soul and Christ as the Bride and Bridegroom, and she confessed to me with great awe that she really believed that Christ had often come to her at night when in bed as the real Bridegroom, and had actually had a bridegroom's connexion with her. She taught this doctrine to a choice circle of friends, and even tried by personal contact to produce in them those physical thrills which she believed were the actual contact of the Holy Ghost. She overawed these friends by the tremendous force of her own convictions, and in many cases obtained what I now believe to have been hypnotic control over them, so that they were not surprised or shocked at anything she said or did, but accepted it all as from God, and as being the avenue through which the Holy Ghost was to be poured out upon them. As far as I knew, however, no one adopted her views, but when the glamour of her presence was removed, they came to their senses and saw that it had all been a dreadful delusion. But even then, although their eyes had been opened to see the fearful errors into which she had led them, none of them could doubt the sincerity of her belief in the divine origin of her strange views and practices. In the course of time, as my interest in this sort of mysticism waned, I lost sight of her, and have never known what the final issue was, although I have reason to believe that her own eyes also must have been at last opened to the mistakes she had made.

In regard to that tent meeting at the camp ground, where she entered into that first wonderful experience, I met a lady about a year afterwards who had been present at first, but who had been called away suddenly and had not heard of Miss S.'s experience. She asked me if I remembered that meeting, and said that she was one of those present who were praying for the Baptism of Spirit, and that while she was praying she seemed to have her spiritual eyes opened. She saw the Holy Ghost in bodily form hovering in the air above the meeting, striving to come down into the hearts of the people present, but an invisible barrier seemed to hinder his approach any nearer than about four feet above our heads, and although he pushed and pushed to get through this barrier seemed impregnable, and he was obliged reluctantly to give up the attempt. She said in her heart, ' Oh, Lord, what does this vision mean ? ' And the reply came, ' It means that all hearts present are so full of themselves that it is impossible for me to find entrance, and it is of no use for people to pray for the

Lord to take possession of them unless they are first emptied of self '.

Now as a fact the person who was acknowledged by all to be the most full of self was my friend, Miss S——, who had apparently received the Baptism. What it was that happened to her, or what the whole thing meant, I was not for many years able to explain, but my opinion now is that, being a very emotional person, her emotions had got worked up to the highest pitch by our prayers and our consecration in the dark, and that what happened to her was simply an overwhelming excitement of her whole emotional nature, and that she did not really receive any greater blessing from God than all the rest of us received, or than would naturally come to souls as earnest and eager as we were.

I must say here that in all my experience of these wonderful outpourings they always happened to emotional people, and were not necessarily accompanied by any increased holiness on the part of the recipients.

I had a neighbour at one time who used to come and see me every day, and fill me with awe and eager longing at the accounts she gave me of the ' waves of glory ' that had swept over her during the previous night, which she believed were the tokens of the manifest presence of the Lord. But at the very same time this friend was so full of self, and so determined to get her own way that she resorted to what often seemed to me dishonest and underhand means to accomplish her ends. She would say after one of these recitals, and we had turned to business again, ' There is no other woman

in the world who is so fitted to rule and guide associations
as I am ; I am the only one who could carry on the
work as it ought to be carried on '. And then she would
proceed to arrange plans and devise methods by which
she was to be kept in power ; plans, that, looking back
upon them now, I can see were neither dignified nor
upright.

CHAPTER IV

THE L. FANATICISM

I N the year 1879 we took a furnished house in Coulter Street, Germantown, for the summer. A lady who lived next door to us had lent her house to some friends who had the reputation of being wonderful Christians, and of having great revelations and remarkable experiences. As I was at that time in search of remarkable experiences, I was exceedingly interested in these people, and very soon made their acquaintance. The head of the household was a Methodist minister named J.L., and I found him to be a most impressive and interesting man. He had a way of suddenly turning to you when conversation was going on and saying that he had a message for you from the Lord, and then giving you some solemn word of warning—that the time had come for you to take a decided step, or something of that sort. There were also in the house two sisters named W., whose father, Dr. W., was a man of position and authority in the Methodist Church, with a great reputation for piety.

Their home was on the Atlantic coast, where they were held in great repute as being people of singular piety and devotion.

From the first I was profoundly impressed by the apparent holiness and devotedness of this household, and felt that they must have been brought there on purpose to help me onward in my earnest search for a realised oneness with Christ, a oneness to which they seemed to have attained in a very marvellous degree.

The thing which interested me at first was the remarkable way in which they seemed to understand the guidance of the Holy Spirit in all the little daily affairs of life. I have spoken of this more especially in my chapter on Divine Guidance, but I must say here that their way of looking continually, moment by moment, to the Lord for His Guidance, and their perfect certainty that He did indeed, according to His promise, direct their every step, seemed to invest them with an atmosphere of holiness and to surround them with the conscious presence of the Lord in a way that made itself felt by everyone who came into their presence. They seemed literally to live and move and have their being in God. And to a soul, hungering as mine was to know the utmost possibilities of the life hid with Christ in God, it seemed that it ought to be almost like entering the very gates of Heaven to be in their presence, and I threw myself with intense eagerness into their teaching and their influence.

No one could associate with them and not believe that they thought themselves special Divine favourites. They professed to be so minutely guided in life that I was very anxious to attain the same experience, so finally I got Miss W. to give me a sample of the way in which she was guided. She said it was like this : that when she was awakened in the morning her first conscious thought was to consecrate the day to the Lord, and to ask Him to guide her every step of the way throughout the whole day. She would then ask Him whether she was to get up or not ; and very often, although it was apparently very important that she should get up, the Lord told her to stay in bed. Then, perhaps, in a few minutes the voice would order her to get up. Then she would proceed to get up. As she put on each article she asked the Lord whether she was to put it on, and very often the Lord would tell her to put on the right shoe and leave off the other ; sometimes she was to put on one stocking and leave off the other ; sometimes she was to put on both stockings and no shoes ; and sometimes both shoes and no stockings ; it was the same with all the articles of dress. She said also that often during the day, when she was seated at work, the Lord would tell her to get up and go out of the room, and when she got out would tell her to come back, And often she would be told to move from one chair to the other, or to go and stand on the front doorstep, or to do all sorts of erratic things. She said that the object of this was to make her pliable so that she would be ready to follow the guidance of the Lord on the instant. I immediately thought that I would like to live in the same way, so the next morning after this conversation I began the process, and it was with the greatest difficulty that I got dressed or downstairs to my duties, as the voice kept telling me to do all sorts of things. Then when I did get downstairs I could hardly get through my breakfast, for the voice would suggest, just as I would get a mouthful nearly into my mouth, that I must not take it. I spent the morning running about from one chair to another, going out to the steps and coming back again, and running from one room to the other, and even going so far as to take off my shoes and stockings, and then to put them on again without any apparent cause.

I kept this up until about twelve o'clock, and then my common sense revolted, and I said to myself, 'There is no Divine guidance in this at all. I have just got the ideas from what Miss W. told me, and I am making it up all out of my own head', and I was forced sorrowfully to conclude that I had not fathomed the secret of Divine guidance yet. This did not, however, weaken my desire to know the inner depths of the experience of which I heard, but gradually I began to discover that I was in the middle of a party of the greatest fanatics that the world contained.

In spite of their evident holiness, I had been conscious all the while of something mysterious about the whole household, an intangible atmosphere of something wrong which seemed to fill the house, and to look out of the eyes of its inmates, and to be heard in the tones of their voices. There was nothing I could lay my hands upon, or could even formulate in my thoughts, and whenever the feeling forced itself upon me I blamed myself as being as yet too unspiritual fully to enter into their heights of spirituality and set myself more determinedly than ever to attain to their divine level. Believing, as they taught, that human reason must be laid aside in spiritual matters, and only the interior voice of the Spirit obeyed, I refused as long as possible to pay any attention to the pricks of the common-sense basis of my nature, and tried to convince myself that I was in this way being uplifted more and more into the secret things of God's immediate presence.

I must confess it was all very fascinating. I know of nothing more delightful than to be living, as it were, on the very threshold of the spiritual region, with apparently only a thin veil between, and with the expectation of the veil being drawn aside at any moment and some wonderful blaze of glory bursting forth to overwhelm one with Divine revelations. Every day during that summer I awakened to a magnificent anticipation, and, if every night I went to bed disappointed, it was only to feel convinced that the expected revelation must surely come the next day.

It is needless to say that nothing of what I expected came to me, but I must confess even after this lapse of time that in many respects their teaching was exceedingly valuable. And I did receive during the course of the summer a real revelation of God that has made life to me a different thing ever since. It came to me, as all my revelations always have come, in the form of a conviction. I wanted a vision, I got a fact ; and a thousand times since I have thanked God it was so, though at the time it seemed but a poor and flat fulfilment of my magnificent anticipations. It came in this wise. It was the continual habit of this strange household to refer everything to God. They seemed to make

Him the centre and circumference, the top and the bottom, the inside and the outside of everything. They never even seemed to recognize that there were or could be such things as second causes, and they were unable to conceive of any question to which God was not a sufficient answer. Their one universal reply to everything was simple, the words, ' Yes ; but then there is God ' ; and no arguments or questionings could turn them from this by so much as a hair's-breadth.

As may be imagined, during my intercourse with them, because of all the unexplainable mystery accompanied by the apparent wonderful holiness that seemed to surround them, I often found myself in a good deal of spiritual perplexity, and, as I looked upon them as religious teachers deserving the highest confidence, I continually went to one or other of them with my difficulties, chiefly, however, to the oldest of the W. sisters, Miss Caroline W., who was a woman of great culture and intelligence and unusual spiritual power. I would pour out to her all my interior perplexities and difficulties and temptations, to which I must say she always listened very patiently, but when I would pause for some comforting or helpful reply, there would always ensue a moment or two of silence, and then she would invariably say in a tone that seemed utterly to conclude the matter, ' Yes, that may all be true, but then, *there is God*.' I used to feel quite impatient with her, for I looked upon myself as a ' very interesting case', and my difficulties as being of a rather unusual and interesting kind, and it seemed to me they really deserved greater consideration and more detailed and definite help than was to be found in the simple assertion that 'there was God.' But my most impassioned or despairing stories of my spiritual woes could never elicit anything more than this. 'Yes, yes,' she would say ; 'I know it all. But then, there is God.' The result of this was that she did succeed by constant reiteration in taking my mind off myself and my perplexities and in bringing me to see that God was enough.

Towards the end of their stay, one night, a friend who had come to sit at their feet and I had gone to bed in great perplexity, full of questioning as to how it could be that God would permit people who wanted to follow Him, and were trying to walk in His paths, to wander into error. We went to sleep in this perplexity, unable to see any light ; but, somehow, in the morning when we met, we turned to each other and said, in the sense that we had never said it before, the single word, 'God !' and with that word came to us a recognition of the all-sufficiency of God in a way that has never left us. From that moment I, personally, have never had any anxiety, any question, any doubt in the religious life that could not be answered at once by the simple repetition of the word 'God', and ever since, whenever we meet, although it has been thirty or forty years—in fact, in all our letters and conversations—we constantly greet one another with the repetition of that one name, the name of God.

It would be impossible to put into words just what seemed to come to us that morning, but it certainly was a satisfying revelation of the all-sufficiency of God, just the bare God—if I might use the expression—for all our needs. And thousands of times since I have had all my perplexities dissipated and all my fears dispelled by the simple repetition of these words, ' God is enough.' And I shall never cease to feel real gratitude to this strange household for having brought me to this, although I very soon found out some dreadful things about them.

As the summer passed I became more and more impressed with the strange and mysterious religious atmosphere which surrounded this household, but the time came when my friend wanted her house back again, and when Mr. L. and his friends returned to their several homes, and I was as much mystified as ever as to what it all meant.

One day, however, shortly after they had gone, I received a telegram from Mrs. C. in Boston, begging me to come and see her at once on a matter of vital importance. The message was so urgent that I took a night train, and arrived there the next morning. Immediately Mrs. C. told me that she thought I ought to know the state of things in this household, and she had sent for me to tell me about it. She brought in a highly respectable woman doctor, who told me the following facts.

The doctor said that she had two very intimate friends in Boston, who were ladies of very good standing, and, in fact, one of them was at the head of a large school, or college, and was considered an authority on education. They were young women of unusual culture and of great refinement and charm, respected by every-body, with a great religious reputation ; and were, in fact, devoted Christians. They had become acquainted with Mr. L., the Methodist minister, who was the head of the mysterious household next door to me, about eighteen months before, and had seemed to find great spiritual uplifting from his teachings. This doctor was at that time in charge of a hospital, and these ladies would often come to see her. She noticed that one of them seemed to be losing her spirits, and to be greatly depressed, with so far as she knew no apparent reason. She seemed to be on the verge all the time of saying something to the doctor which she appeared afraid to continue, and the doctor felt that her friend had a confidence to make to her which for some reason she was reluctant to make.

One night this friend came to stay all night at the hospital and slept in the room with the doctor. As she was standing by the looking-glass arranging her hair, the doctor noticed something peculiar in her appearance, and it flashed across her mind that her friend was in the family way. She exclaimed, ' Oh, darling, what is the matter ? ' and her friend burst into tears. Nothing more was said ; the doctor was too shocked to speak ; she would as soon have expected to find the Angel Gabriel in such a plight as her friend ; and they spent the night both weeping, but saying nothing till towards the morning. Then her friend opened her heart and confided in the doctor. She told her that she and her companion had been greatly impressed by the teaching of this Mr. L., to whom they had been introduced by Miss ——, a religious teacher of a great deal of spirituality, living in Boston. They both became greatly influenced by Mr. L's teaching, and gradually he had unfolded to them that it had been revealed to him that he was to be the father of a race of children that were to be born into the world as Christ was, and that the Lord had shown him that they themselves were to be the favoured mothers of these children. Whether he was a bad man or simply a wild fanatic I have never been able to decide, but at all events he succeeded in completely deluding these ladies, and in carrying out his purposes, and this poor thing was now expecting to be the mother of one of these children. The agonies of mind that she had gone through could not be described. She dared not admit the idea that it was a delusion, for her whole spiritual life seemed to depend upon believing that she had been rightly guided ; for if she could think that in the most solemn moments of consecration the Lord could allow her to be so deceived, she would feel that she could never trust Him again. She clung with a deathlike grip to the belief that it was Divine guidance, and that she was greatly favoured to be allowed to be the mother of one of these wonderful children. How to get through the earthly part of it, however, was the great difficulty. But her doctor friend stepped in to the rescue ; she took a house out of the city, brought her friend there, took care of her until the time came, carried her safely through her confinement and kept the facts hidden from everybody.

The lady had told her mother, who had been anxious about her health, that she was broken down by so much teaching, and was going to the country for a complete rest, and there was no exposure.

Mr. L. was a constant visitor at the house, as the doctor had not the heart to plunge her friend into the abyss of despair which would have been her portion if she had lost faith in him. The doctor did not like his ways at all, and herself believed that it was pure human lust. However, the thing was carried through ; the doctor adopted the baby, and her friend went back to her usual avocations. She never lost her delusion during my knowledge of her. Mr. L. married the other lady, the companion who had shared in her delusion, and, soon after the birth of the baby the mother went to live with him and his wife, and for many years they formed one household.

The dear sister who had lent Mr. L. the house and who was considered by us the greatest saint of all, came so much under his influence in the end that I began to feel afraid she would give up everything and go and live with him. She was a wealthy widow, and I began to feel sure that he wanted to get her money. I made her promise, therefore, that if he came to see her and she was tempted to go away with him, that she would send for me and my husband to come out and consult. And one night we received a telegram : ' Mr. L. is here ; come out '.

We dropped everything and went, and sure enough L. was there, and had almost succeeded in persuading her to put all her private property into his hands, and go and live with him. We at once, in his presence, told her the whole story as we had heard it, and while he acknowledged the facts, he stuck to his position that he was commissioned of the Lord to bring forth these children, and that they were not begotten according to any natural process. We succeeded, however, in frightening him so much as to revelations that might be made, that he himself told our friend he did not believe she was called to go with him ; and Mrs. ——— never ceased to thank us for her deliverance. How many poor souls were beguiled during that strange summer I do not know.

Of course, from that time my intercourse with these dear misguided Christians ceased, but about a year after I received a very impressive and solemn note from one of them saying that the way was still open for me to return to the Lord if I would give up my self-will and consent to be guided as the Lord led. I had, however, by this time been enlightened as to the fact that all these fancied revelations were really delusions, and that while these dear people might be honestly trying to serve the Lord, they were certainly being led into very disastrous fanaticism, and I replied to this effect. Since then, I have neither seen nor heard about them. I had appealed to Miss W. if ever she saw the error of her ways to let me know, and as I have never received any word, I presume she still continues in her delusions.

CHAPTER V

THE BAPTISM OF THE SPIRIT

OWING to the fact of my being so tremendously in
earnest in my search after the deep things of
God, I think rumours of my willingness to listen and
to learn must have got spread abroad, for it really
seemed to me that everybody with any sort of a ' remarkable experience ' came to pour it into my ears, and I
often wonder whether there can be any phase of religious
experience of which I have not heard. During the time
of my search I think all the fanatics in the United States
must have found their way to my presence to try and
draw me into their especial net, and as I was always
ready to listen sympathetically, hoping that among them
all I might at last find the truth, they were often led on
to reveal to me their inmost secrets.

I confess I was at that time a very easily gulled
person, and was inclined to believe everything that was
told me, and to accept the most absurd experiences as
being of Divine origin and worthy of consideration,
if only the narrator would assert it strongly enough.
Especially could I be completely taken in by anyone
who professed to be 'guided by the Lord'. This was
owing, I expect, to my early Quaker teaching about
Divine Guidance. People had only to say to me
that the Lord had led them into such or such a course,

for me to bow down before them in profound reverence. I confess my common sense often received a severe shock, but this was always attributed to my lack of spirituality, and I was made to believe that when I arrived at a deeper insight I should be able to understand the Divine reasons for what at the time seemed to me violations of good sense and even of simple morality. To a soul as hungry after God as mine, anything that seemed to promise a revelation from Him was welcomed, in spite of past disappointments, with an ever freshly springing hope and enthusiasm.

No one who has not been within the charmed circle of mysticism can possibly know the fascination of exploring these unseen spiritual realities where you feel that at any moment some unexpected glory may be revealed to you. Nor can any outsider understand how easy it is to abandon one's common sense and right reason and yield to the plausible enticements of one's emotional nature, which is always in these circumstances unduly active and fervent. Having known something of the fascination I speak of, I cannot but wonder that anyone who enters upon this mystic pathway escapes unscathed, and I can never be thankful enough for the bottom stratum of practical common sense in my nature that always seemed to drag me back when I was in danger of wandering too far.

But because I sympathized, a great deal more was poured out to me, I am convinced, than would generally be the case. On this account, after I had found out for myself the danger of it all, I was able to help some of the poor victims who had been caught in the toils, and could see no hope or comfort anywhere.

A young woman came to me once in the greatest anguish of spirit because of a snare into which she had been led. She said she had been seeking the Baptism of the Spirit as a result of the fervent preaching of a Methodist minister in the town where she lived, and had found great spiritual help from her conversations with him. They found, she said, that when they were together they seemed to feel an especial nearness to the Lord, and the closer they sat together the more they felt it. They constantly, when in one another's company, had wonderful waves of divine thrills going through them, especially when there was any personal contact, which thrills the preacher told her were the conscious Baptism of the Holy Spirit for which she was praying. Of course, if this was the case, the more of these waves of delicious thrills they had the more truly filled with the Spirit they were, and they had consequently sought every opportunity of being together, and had encouraged a closer and closer personal contact, never dreaming of evil, until at last she found herself in the midst of a criminal connection with the preacher who was already a married man. This had awakened her with a rude shock and she was in despair. Could it be, she asked herself, that the Lord had permitted her to fall into sin when she was so earnestly striving after holiness, or was it because she had an impure mind and had had impure thoughts of what was really the truest spiritual purity. Her distress of mind had nearly driven her crazy, and having heard of me as a religious teacher she had come to see if I could help her. She entreated me to tell her what was right and what she was to do. Fortunately by this time I had discovered that all such things were dangerous deceptions, and I was able to explain the whole matter to this poor girl, and to convince her that her only course was immediately and for ever to give up all intercourse of every kind with the preacher who had led her into these fearful delusions. It was pathetic to witness the agony and distress of this poor deluded girl. She said that she thought someone ought to stand on the steeple-top of every town and tell everybody in the town the danger that lay in this sort of thing. She followed my advice and gave up the intercourse, but the strain had been too much for her and not long after, happily, she died.

A year or two after that summer when Mr. L. and his mysterious household lived next door to us, I was in Boston, and was asked if I could not go to see the lady who had been largely instrumental in starting people, and especially the young women I have mentioned in my account of the L. fanaticism, on the career which led them to L. It was hoped I might perhaps help her to see how wrong it all was, as it was feared she might lead other young women into similar pathways. I found her to be a quiet refined lady rather past middle age, evidently very intelligent and a Christian worker who was highly esteemed by all who knew her. I told her what I knew about the L. household and asked her if she could defend it. She said, yes, she could—

that the Lord's leadings were often very mysterious and such as the natural man could not understand, but that what God had pronounced clean no one might dare to call unclean, and that these dear saints had been most manifestly led by Him. All my expostulations were met with the assertion, made evidently in real honesty, that she had been led into these courses and that she could do nothing but obey ; and I may as well say here that when people say they are ' led ' it is of no earthly use to reason with them. The Divine authority that they think they have for their course naturally outweighs any human influence. During the course of my conversation with this lady she said : ' You may think it strange, Mrs. Smith, but I speak from experience ; there have been times when, in order to help my friends to receive the Baptism of the Holy Spirit, I have felt distinctly led of the Lord to have them get into bed with me and lie back to back without any nightgown between. And ', she added, ' it has always brought to them the conscious Baptism '.

I expressed my horror at this and tried to show her how dangerous it was and to what abuses it might lead, and she seemed to begin to see it, but she exclaimed, ' Oh, Mrs. Smith, I dare not look at it in that light or I shall lose all my faith in God. What *am* I to do if in my most sacred moments, when I am most consecrated to God, and most fully abandoned to His will, the command comes to me to do this sort of thing ? How can I believe that at such moments He would let me be deluded into evil, and how can I refuse to obey His voice ? ' It was a hard question to answer, but I could only reiterate over and over that it was all a delusion of evil spirits, and beg her to give it up. I never shall forget the pitiful pathos of it all, nor the despairing way in which she replied to all my expostulations. ' I dare not doubt ! I dare not doubt ! ' And there I had to leave her ; and I have never heard since what became of her. But I know positively that she has been the means of leading a great many young women into the same line of things.

Another friend of mine to whom I had told about Dr. R. and his views, received while I was talking to her, what she believed was the Baptism, and began to experience right then and there thrills of rapture from head to foot, which completely carried her away. She went on for many months in the joy of this experience, feeling that every moment when she did not have these thrills of rapture was a wasted moment, and she used to spend most of her time lying on the sofa trying to induce them to come. She also became very fanatical, and felt it her duty to kiss several men, with the idea that through that means God would bestow either great blessings upon them or greater blessings upon herself. She had felt led to kiss Mr. L. during the summer that he lived next door to me, and years afterwards it came upon her again. It is a form that fanaticism is very apt to take, and especially feeling led to kiss men whom it is a trial to kiss. And this dear friend of mine, who was by nature the very last person to do any such thing, and who was so good and pure minded that we all

called her ' Saint Sarah ', began to have this unfortunate
' leading '. She was impressed with the idea that
through this performance God would bestow the Baptism
of the Spirit upon the recipient of her kisses. At one
of our meetings at Brighton, when there was a great
deal of talk about the Baptism of the Spirit, and many
souls were hungering for it, our host, a refined and cultured gentleman over middle age, expressed a great
desire to realize this experience for himself. My friend,
' Saint Sarah ', heard him speaking about it, and I
noticed that she became very confused and embarrassed
in her manner, and shortly after left the room. A little
later I went to her about some matter, and she confided
to me that she felt led to kiss him herself as a means
of imparting to him the Baptism of the Holy Ghost.
She was in the greatest trouble about it, and said she
did not see how it would be possible for her to do it.
She was already considerably past middle age, and she
felt that she would be making herself ridiculous. I
told her I was sure it was all a delusion, and did everything
I could to drive the notion out of her mind. But it was
useless. Days went on and she became really ill with
the conflict ; and at last, seeing that there was no way
out of it but for her to do it, I said, ' It won't hurt ; I'll
explain it to him. So just go and kiss him and be done
with it ! ' My taking it in this way greatly relieved her
mind. I told our host what she wanted to do, and he
said he wouldn't object in the least. He had the sense
to see that while it was only a vagary of her mind, she
could not be at rest until she had carried it out. We

felt so sorry for her distress of mind that we arranged that she should kiss him in the presence of his wife. This set her mind entirely at rest, and she was able to perform what she thought was her religious duty. This kiss was given and no harm came of it, but I must add, no baptism for the recipient either !

One would have supposed that this would have caused her to doubt all such leadings, but this was not the case. In two or three other instances the same process was repeated, but never with any result.

This dear Saint was so enamoured of what she called the 'Touch of God', that she spent a large part of her time seeking for it and enjoying it, until it finally became a sort of possession, and in the end brought about the very sad, but alas! not uncommon, hallucination that the devil was her bridegroom and actually lived inside her body. For several months she was nearly out of her mind. What had plunged her into this deep depression was the fact that she had sent her handwriting to a lady who professed to be able to read handwritings—a very good Christian lady she was, who said she had spiritual insight into handwriting—and when she had read this handwriting she said it was the handwriting of a person who was possessed of a devil. My friend believed it, and it precipitated her into the deepest agony of sorrow, with the result, as I have said above, that she thought the devil was an actual inhabitant of her body. I was away from America at that time. When I returned and found the state of mind she was in, I did my best to combat it, but found it impossible to make any impression. She would not even allow me to mention the name of God, and when I did she would shrink in the utmost horror. She thought that, as she was inhabited by the devil, the name of God was something that she could not bear. I made up my mind that she must be freed from this somehow, so I took some of her writing and went to the woman who had plunged her into the trouble and told her the dreadful effects of her former words, and said to her, ' And now you must give me in writing the assurance that the devil has gone out of her,' and I bullied her into doing it. I then went back to my friend armed with this assurance, and said to her : ' Now the devil has gone out of thee, and here is the proof '. She believed it, and from that moment began to recover, and has since lived a peaceful and normal Christian life.

CHAPTER VI

JERUSALEM FANATICISM

I HAVE made during the course of my life a pretty thorough study in fanaticism, and think that I know all the ins and outs of it, and I feel towards it very much like a person who has been exceedingly interested in a Punch and Judy show, till they find out how the puppets are worked, and after that have lost their interest.

My first introduction to fanaticism, if I leave out all that I got from the Quakers to start with, which was a good deal, came through the Methodist doctrine of entire sanctification. That doctrine has been one of the greatest blessings of my life, but it has also introduced me into an emotional region where common sense has no chance, and where everything goes by feelings and voices and impressions. One of the first instances I knew definitely was a dear beloved saint, an old maid of about sixty, who had given up everything in life to follow the Lord, and who was considered by everybody who knew her to be one of the saints of the earth. She was even so saintlike that she wouldn't tie a bow in her bonnet strings, but had a hook and eye to meet under her chin. She was not a Quaker, but she had all the Quaker scruples with regard to dress, and looked as she walked about like the embodiment of ascetic piety. I greatly revered her and sat at her feet to be taught.

One day, shortly after a New Year's season, a friend who like myself was seeking after light, accompanied me on a visit to this dear saint, in order to learn some spiritual lessons, and we expected great enlightenment. We asked her to tell us her last experience. She said that at the New Year's time which had just passed, she had told the Lord that she wanted to make Him some New Year's gift, and that as she had given Him everything that she possessed and everything she was, she could not think of anything new to give. Then, she said, the Lord told her that there was one thing, and that was her virginity, and that He would send a man whom she must be willing to receive in His name and surrender herself to him. She told us that she had said, ' Thy will be done ', and was now awaiting the ringing of the bell and the advent of the promised man.

My friend and I were horrified, but as this dear lady was deaf, and we had to shout in talking to her, we could not scream our disapproval and horror, and could only listen in silence and leave as soon as possible.

When we got out of the door, we looked at each other, and I said, ' Mary H., did that woman really say these things ? ' and she said, ' Hannah Smith, did she ? ' I confess that neither of us would have believed that it really had taken place, had we not been able to confirm one another.

After we got home I wrote the dear lady a letter, and told her that I believed she was under the delusion of evil spirits, and that I hoped she would review her position and give it all up, and said that until she did I should be obliged to stop being friends with her. Many years have elapsed since then, and I have never had a word of retraction, nor have I ever laid eyes on her again. I suppose, therefore, that she still holds her delusion, but whether the man ever came or not, I do not know. I have heard, however, that at one of the camp meeting grounds, where she had a cottage and where she held meetings, the authorities had been obliged to close her meetings on account of the dangerous tendency of her teaching.

I had had an experience previously with this same lady which had partly opened my eyes. We were all at a Camp Meeting together, and I went into her tent one morning to see her. Her Bible was lying open on her bed with a list of texts on a slip of paper, and to while away the time until she returned, I looked out these texts. They were texts about people doing very curious things ; for instance, one Prophet who ate dung at the command of the Lord ; another who slept with a harlot at the command of the Lord, etc. It appeared that she had been finding out from the Bible what would be the most awful things to do, and using them as encouragements to any form of fanaticism that might suggest itself.

Abandonment to the Lord often seems to lead to strange things. One of the strangest instances I know was the Jerusalem party. I first heard of it in this way : I had gone to Chicago to hold a series of meetings. It was just in the midst of my researches into these fanatical experiences, not researches of curiosity, but researches based on an honest desire to get some light, on what I thought the mystical way of approaching God. By my Quaker education, I was exceedingly inclined towards mysticism, and the books I had read—such as Madame Guyon, Fénelon, Isaac Pennington and others, all of which lead to a life of introspection and self-abandonment—had greatly strengthened me in this, so that I honestly believed that wonderful spiritual light would come, and did come, to souls that gave themselves up to the control of their interior emotions and followed impressional guidance.

When I went to Chicago I left behind a most interesting circle of these mystics, and said to myself, ' I shall not see any of these dear mystics while I am in Chicago ', because Chicago did not seem to me a place that could breed mystics. But, at the close of the very first meeting I held, a party of two or three men and two or three women came up to me and said that the Lord had sent them to make a revelation to me. I was delighted, and was all ears to hear what they had to say. They said it was a long story, and they must come to the place where I was staying to have a private interview. I arranged for this, and looked forward to it with the greatest interest and hope of receiving light. I should say that they were people of good social standing and of great religious reputation and very earnest in good works ; in fact, one of them, a Chicago lawyer, had worked with Mr. Moody, while his wife had been famous for the wonderful way in which she had borne the loss of all her children on the wreck of the ' Ville de Havre ', a ship that had gone down in mid-ocean under peculiarly dreadful circumstances. Another one was a lady who was at the head of all the religious movements in the town, and who was looked up to by every one. They were all past middle age, and were people of intelligence as well as piety. They told me the following story : that one of their number, a Mrs. L., a charming lady, whose husband had held some official position in Washington, and who had been socially prominent, who knew very little about religion, but was eager to know more about it, had the previous summer been attending a methodist camp meeting which was held in the neighbourhood of where they were residing. At one of the meetings some exceedingly interesting experiences were told concerning what was called ' The Baptism of the Holy Spirit', and her soul was fired with the desire to have the same experience for herself. Being very ignorant of all religious methods, she did not know how to get it, but as she sat in her seat, she held out her hand and said, ' Now, Lord, you know how ignorant I am, and you know how much I want this experience, and now I hold out my hand to receive it. Please give it to me'. Immediately she felt a thrill of delight pass through her, and the feeling as of a delightful electric shock all over her body, and fully believed that that was the gift she had been asking for. She then said, ' Now, Lord, I mean to go by Thy guidance, and as I am so ignorant, please give me a tangible sign by which I shall always know what Thy will is'. Immediately the Lord gave what she believed to be the sign, which was that her lower jaw was cracked up against her upper jaw with a loud crack, and she understood that whenever that crack occurred it was to be taken as the affirmative expression of the Lord's will, with regard to the thing in hand, whatever it might be. She immediately went home and began family worship that night. She asked the Lord to show her where to read. She took the Bible and ran her finger down the different books, and when she came to the book that she was to read her jaw cracked. She then turned to the book and ran her finger over the chapters, and in the same way she was told what chapter she was to read by the cracking of her jaw. She then ran her finger over the verses and began to read when her jaw cracked and stopped reading when it cracked again. And in this way she believed that she had read exactly what the Lord wanted her to read, neither more nor less. Of course this opened up most enchanting possibilities of a life of guidance, and she began to regulate her whole life by the cracking of her jaw.

Very soon other people were attracted by this remarkable phenomenon, and began to come to her for guidance in their lives. A little community gathered round her, who all brought everything in their lives to be tested by the cracking of her jaw. They engaged or dismissed servants, arranged their households, transacted their business, gave up old businesses, entered into new businesses, formed friendships, gave up friends, dressed—

did everything in fact by the guidance of this sign. But, as the cracking was very loud, it became unpleasant to her husband, especially as it would often take place in the very middle of a meal, so she prayed the Lord that He would please give her a quieter sign, and her prayer was answered by the cracking of the jaw being stopped and the sign being transferred to her eyes, which were drawn back into the head, as if by strings fastened behind and pulled by an invisible hand. From that time, everything was tested by the drawing in of her eyes. This was only an affirmative sign ; when the answer was 'no', there was no sign given.

The community in Chicago gradually increased. One after another was drawn into it, and they established a place of meeting a little out of Chicago, in a suburb, and met there on Sunday, when, among other things, the sign told them that they were to use oranges for their communion service.

All this they told me, with the assurance that the Lord had revealed to them that *I* was to join their community. I was charmed with the people, and was deeply interested in their experiences, but did not feel at that time prepared to join the community. Not very long afterwards, when I had returned home, I received a letter from Mrs. L. saying that the Lord by her sign had revealed to them that they were to go and form a colony in Jerusalem, and that on their way they were to stop at our house and pick me up to go with them. They came, a party of about twelve, and spent two or three days with us. They told me that the Lord had revealed to them that He was coming very soon, and that they must be in Jerusalem to meet Him, that they were the Elect Bride and would be the only ones in the world who would be prepared for His coming. The day after they arrived in Jerusalem the Star of Bethlehem was to come and settle on the head of one of them, and this fact would go out to the world, and immediately all the people who were expecting the Lord's coming, and looking for it, would hasten as fast as possible to Jerusalem and gather round the Star, and then, when all the saints were gathered, the Lord would ascend, and His saints with Him, into the air above Jerusalem.

We had a most interesting visit from them, but I made the discovery that I could control the sign, and consequently I somewhat lost my confidence in it ! As an illustration, I asked Mrs. L. to take a drive with me. She immediately retired into herself, and asked the Lord whether she was to go. Her eyes were not drawn in and consequently she answered 'No', that she was not allowed to go. I made up my mind she should go, so I took no special notice of this answer, but I put my will into the matter and began to talk to her in a careless sort of way about the beauties of Wissakickon Creek. By this means, I excited her imagination, and in a little while I again gave my invitation for the drive with the inward determination that her eyes should be drawn in. And they were, and we took our drive, which she greatly enjoyed.

She was at this time, by means of her sign, writing a

new Bible. One of the party was the scribe, and whenever the inspiration came upon her to write it was preceded by all sorts of curious jerkings of her body. Her knees would come up to her face ; her hands would be jerked in all sorts of directions ; and her body would be twisted all round, and her eyes would be drawn in so energetically that you would think they would never come out again. She would then begin in a slow and unnatural voice something as follows :

' I—the—Lord—speak—in—these—days—through —the—mouth—of—my—servant—Moses—to —give — you —the—fresh—and —present—revelation—of — my—will—', etc., etc.

I was exceedingly interested in the writing of this new Bible, and as the inspiration did not seem to come upon her often enough to please me, I made up my mind to try and bring it on. The method I adopted was putting my will into it and then putting my hand to my face and bowing my head in perfect silence. Naturally the same silence fell upon all the company, as it is really difficult to continue conversation when one member of the company seems to be in meditation. The result always was that in a few minutes the inspiration would come upon her ; the jerking would begin, and some of the Bible would be dictated.

Their visit lasted several days, and much of the time was spent by the ladies in their own rooms, altering their dresses to meet the requirements of the 'sign'. They told me that they were determined to take me with them, and they asked me if I believed in the guidance of the Spirit, and when I said yes, they told me that if I was faithful to this interior guide I would as certainly accompany them to Jerusalem as the sun would rise the next day. However, my common sense asserted itself, and when the time came I did not go.

Needless to say I have watched their career in Jerusalem with the greatest interest, and I am sorry to say that nothing has turned out as they expected. No Star of Bethlehem came and settled on their heads ; the Lord did not come according to their prophecies. Dear Mrs. L., who with her sign was the founder of the whole thing, has been deposed, and another member of the party has been promoted to the place of leader. What her sign was, or whether she had any at all, I do not know.

After two or three years had passed, I wrote to them, reminding them of the fact that they had had a revelation that I was to go with them, and saying that they must be convinced now that their revelations were not infallible, as I not only had not gone with them, but was doing all in my power to keep people away from them and all similar fanaticisms. They replied that the prophecy was still true, and that they were told by the Lord that I should yet join them.

CHAPTER VII

THE H. FANATICISM

ONE of the most prominent fanatics with whom I have been thrown in contact was Thomas Harris, a great mystic, and yet, I fear, a very fallible human being. His story was this. He was a preacher in New York, and was very much impressed with the fact that neither he himself, nor anyone he knew, lived up to what he believed to be the Christian ideal. He made up his mind to separate himself from everything in the world, and devote himself to cultivating his spiritual nature, and to seeking after spiritual knowledge, and to living a life fully in accord with what he believed to be the teachings of Christ. One morning in his congregation he told them of his struggles, and asked if there were any in that congregation who would join him in his decision to give up the world and devote themselves to the spiritual life. About ten members rose, and they began from that time to meet for prayer and consecration, and in a little while they formed a small community and cut themselves off from all ordinary life in order the better to give themselves up to what they believed were the teachings of the spirit. They seemed to acquire great spiritual power, and to receive great spiritual blessings, and believed that they were directly taught in a peculiar manner by the Lord. They gradually withdrew more and more from the world, and gave themselves up more and more to this inward teaching, and in the end became fanatics of the deepest dye.

At the time I first became acquainted with Mr. Harris and his community, they were settled in California, and had built themselves a house according to what they believed to be the Divine direction sent them from Heaven. Among other things, I remember it had no separate rooms nor doors, but simply little recesses where beds were placed, because in the new order of things their ideal was that there was to be no need for secrecy, but every one could be open and above board with all they did. They got the idea that the present order of things was to come very shortly to an end and that a new order, which they called the Arch-Natural, was to be introduced, in which everything and everybody would be pure and holy. I do not think that this was to be Heaven, but it was to be a sort of stepping-stone to Heaven, in which present material things were to pass away, but a new order of material things was to exist. They thought, for instance, that their house having been built by Divine direction was an arch-natural house, and therefore would exist through the coming change. They lived there in a community which apparently was all innocence, but which, underneath, contained a great many of the frailties of human nature, and especially in regard to the sexes. In fact, they were said to practise, *under Divine direction always,* a species of free love. One of their great ideas was that each person had somewhere in the universe a spiritual counterpart, who was their true mate, and that the aim of everyone should be so to abstract themselves from the world and worldly relations as to lay hold of this counterpart. It never happened that the earthly husband or wife was the counterpart, consequently those who entered this community were all required to separate from one another, and each to seek his or her counterpart in spiritual regions. They declared that these counterparts assumed an arch-natural body which was visible to the eye and tangible to the touch, and even that there were born arch-natural children who could appear and disappear at will. One would have thought that these doctrines could have found no support from any human being with a grain of common sense, but Mr. Harris was such a wonderful teacher and possessed so much spiritual or magnetic or hypnotic power that he succeeded in inducing even intelligent people and very devoted Christians to adopt his views. I happened to know several of these, and I can truly say that they were among the most delightful and apparently consecrated Christians I knew. With my usual faculty for being deeply interested in all this line of things, and yet being preserved by a small modicum of common sense from personally entering into them, I made quite a study of this phase of fanaticism and twice went to their ' arch-natural ' house to see Mr. Harris. Although he very rarely saw visitors, he consented to see me on both occasions. He told me that he was so sensitive to other people's atmosphere, and the majority of people were so surrounded by a corrupt atmosphere that it made him ill to meet them, and he took me upstairs and showed me a room surrounded with marble wash basins and running streams of water led there from a high spring on the estate where he told me he and his disciples had to come and wash out, or off, the corruptions that they were continually imbibing from the people who came near them. I suspect now that the reason that he imbibed no corruption from me was because he thought I was well off, and would probably add to the finances of the community, as they were entirely supported by the money that was brought in by rich disciples. I knew, for instance, of several cases where people who had read the writings, and who wanted to join them were not allowed to do so, but when, as now and then happened, these people received legacies, or entered into possession of money, immediately the call came to them to join the community. I confess that my judgment of the high spirituality of Mr. Harris was very much modified by the way in which he praised *me* and seemed to imply that *I* was far on in the spiritual life, for I thought that if I was far on, the heights to which he had attained could not be very remarkable. He was very sure that I was going to join his community, and told me that when ' the change ' came, no matter what part of the world I was in, I should at once take the train and come as fast as possible to this house of his which, he said, had been built in the ' arch-natural order ', and would survive the ' change '. His ideas of the arch-natural

world were after all only a higher sort of materialism.
He told me that in that world when you wanted anything
—fish, for instance—you would walk beside a river and
pick up a fish, and hold it in your hands, and imbibe
its life principle without hurting it, and put it back
in the water again. He said also that in that world, if
you lacked any virtue, you would make bread impregnated with that virtue, as, for instance, bread of honesty,
or bread of kindness, and so on, and would eat that
bread, and in this way become honest and kind. But
I do not remember his telling me how the bread was
to be impregnated with these virtues. He also told me
that he had the power of creating arch-natural food,
that he could make cake in his mouth, which could
be taken out and eaten by anyone who wished. He
said that Martha and Mary often paid him visits in
their arch-natural form, and he had many long conversations with them, and that Christ also came in arch-
natural form as a young carpenter with his tools over
his back. He believed that he himself often left his
body and visited distant stars, his body meanwhile
lying in bed in an apparently lifeless condition. His
principal place of visitation, he said, was Mars, which
was going through great changes, and his help was
needed there. He seemed honestly to believe all these
things, and I could see no trace of insanity in him ;
but, in looking back, it seems to me now that the man
must have been out of his mind to talk such nonsense.
One thing I did not like about him ; he wanted to sit
too close to me, and the day I spent with him he would

scarcely leave my side for a moment, and even accompanied me to the station and sat close beside me waiting for the train to come. He said in explanation, ' I find, Mrs. Smith, that great waves of renewed life go through me when I am near you, and I am invigorated and strengthened, instead of being depleted, which is generally the case when I meet other people '. I could not feel that this was any great spiritual experience on his part, but was decidedly of the flesh, and I confess I was thankful to get away. I took good care never to see him again, and I never tried to investigate his teaching afterwards.

CHAPTER VIII

THE L.O. FANATICISM

I KNEW personally a great deal about one of the most prominent of the disciples of Mr. Harris, Laurence Oliphant. Mr. Harris told me, in one of my visits to him, that Laurence Oliphant came to his Community in California a perfect wreck from a life of dissipation, that he tended him and restored him to bodily and spiritual health. Laurence Oliphant himself has told the story of his discipleship elsewhere, but one of the features of it was, as I remember, that he, a gentleman born and bred, was put at once by Mr. Harris to stable work when he joined their community, in order, as Mr. Harris said, that a return to nature and association with animals might purify him of the evils of civilized life. For years he was a most faithful disciple of Mr. Harris, and during this discipleship he came over to England and married a charming Miss Lestrange, a beautiful girl of wealth and position. He imbued her with his views, and took her back with him to the community in California. There Mrs. Oliphant was put to menial work for her purification, and in a very little while Mr. Harris declared that she and her husband were not true counterparts, and he sent her away to teach in a distant city and would not allow them to live together. And afterwards he sent for her to return to the community, and then, in order to separate them, sent Oliphant away on a distant mission. Meanwhile he discovered that Mrs. Oliphant was his own counterpart. To what lengths they went I never knew, but I imagine it was a species of free love.

Finally, Mr. and Mrs. Oliphant revolted from Mr. Harris and left the community, but they found it impossible to recover the money they had put into it, and there was a violent quarrel on the subject. How it ended I never heard, but each party told the most dreadful tales of the other to anybody who would listen. Mr. Harris told me that Mrs. Oliphant during the last part of her stay with him was actually possessed by the devil in bodily presence, and that she used to come into his room in the dead of night and stand at the foot of his bed and tell him that the devil was her lover, and that therefore she could control the whole world, for the devil would do whatever she told him. He said you could fairly see the devil looking out of her eyes, and that he lived in fear and trembling till she left him. I never heard Mrs. Oliphant's side of the story, so cannot tell how the matter looked to her, but Mr. and Mrs. Oliphant, when they left the community, did not give up their fanaticism. They went to Palestine, bought a property, and established a community of their own there. Very remarkable things are reported to have gone on at that community, and finally it had to be closed at the instance of the Vigilance Association of London, which threatened a complete exposure if it continued. Curiously enough, I met in France Madame

C., the wife of Marshal C., who was a great public character there. She told me that she was a devoted follower of Mr. and Mrs. Oliphant, and that she was living in hopes of being summoned by them to join their community. She told me that Mrs. Oliphant was doing a wonderful missionary work among the Arabs in imparting to them what the Oliphants called ' Sympneumata ', which they claimed was the coming of the spiritual counterpart to the individual. She said the way Mrs. Oliphant accomplished this was by getting into bed with these Arabs, no matter how degraded or dirty they were, and the contact of her body brought about, as she supposed, the coming of the counterpart. It was a great trial to her to do this, and she felt that she was performing a most holy mission. As she was one of the most refined and cultivated of English ladies, it is evident that nothing but a strong sense of duty could have induced her to such a course. A great many refined people from England joined the Oliphant's community. What became of them after the breaking up of the community, or what condition it is in now, I have never heard. Mrs. Oliphant, happily, died. After her death and the breaking up of the community, Mr. Oliphant went to Paris, where he continued the propaganda of his peculiar views. One day, when I was living in London, a lady called on me, begging for a confidential interview. She told me the following sorrowful story. She said that she had been an art-student in Paris and had met and become engaged to be married to a young Scottish art-student belonging to a very wealthy Scottish family. This young man, although at the time she did not know it, was a disciple of Mr. Oliphant, and very soon after their engagement he began to talk to her about the wonderful religion that he had got, and introduced her to Mr. Oliphant. She was profoundly impressed by the apparent spirituality of Mr. Oliphant, and by the wonderful mystery of his teaching, and very soon became herself a disciple and set herself to understand this new and strange religion. Very soon, she said, Mr. Oliphant began to take personal liberties with her, and although she was very much surprised and shocked, she felt such confidence in his extreme spirituality and such reverence for him as a teacher, that she concluded it must be her own want of spirituality that caused her to be shocked at what he assured her was the Divine method of propagating the truth. He took more and more liberties with her, and at last induced her to share his bed, with the idea that the personal touch would bring about the sympneumata for which she so longed. She grew more and more uneasy, feeling that this could not be the Divine method, and feeling also that there was a great deal of the flesh in it. Finally, when he thought the time was ripe, he began to urge her to spread the blessing by herself enticing young men into the same relations with her as his own. This was really more than she could bear, and she had at last gone over to America to consult her brother, who was a clergyman in Boston. She told him the whole story, and he assured her it was all of the flesh, and that, in short, it was a species of free love.

She was convinced, and went back to Paris to try to extricate her lover from this terrible snare, but she found it impossible : the hold that Oliphant had upon him was so great that no words of hers had any influence, and she was reluctantly obliged to break off the engagement and return to Boston to escape the malign influence that surrounded her. Her lover continued to be a steadfast disciple of Oliphant's. It was a heartfelt grief to his father, who, although he did not know the deep, inner facts of the case, still realized that his only son and heir was being degraded and ruined by his association with Oliphant.

Mr. Oliphant's idea was that the sexual passion was the only real spiritual life, and that in order to be spiritually alive you must continually keep that passion excited. The consequence was that he himself could never write anything except when his passions were aroused. His influence over this young Scotchman was so great that he had induced him to believe entirely in this theory, and he too was never happy for a single moment unless his own passions were excited.

Then Oliphant, in the course of time, after his wife's death, married an American lady, the daughter of a spiritualist and who was herself a great spiritualist. He shortly developed cancer of the lungs and died a most painful death. His widow, a little while after, married the young Scotchman, who still adhered to their fortunes, and settled with him at Haifa, the place which had been the scene of Mr. Oliphant's special labours. Two years later as he was returning from a voyage to Beyrouth, suddenly, without any warning, the young Scotchman jumped overboard and was drowned. The cause of this I never heard, but I could not but suppose that the poor fellow had gone crazy as the result of all his fanaticism or else had discovered his fatal mistakes. From that time I have heard nothing, either of his widow or of any of the persons connected with his party. Curiously enough there came to spend a few weeks at a cottage near our house in the country a young man who was the son of one of Mr. Oliphant's women disciples. He himself had no interest whatever in the doctrines taught ; he had been born and brought up in the Harris community in California, and he resented bitterly the fact that his boyhood had been passed in washing dishes and doing kitchen-work, and that he had not been allowed to receive any education. He had at last been forced, in order to escape, to run away penniless from the community, and had had a great struggle to give himself an education and find some work in life. He did not seem to know the inner depths of things, but he fully realized that the whole scheme was contrary to common sense and subversive of any possible right living.

On one occasion I was invited to go with two friends of mine, to spend a night at a house in Dorking in order to meet Mr. Oliphant. It was a handsome house and grounds, and there was a large family of a mother and several grown-up daughters ; the father happened to be away from home. In the evening, after dinner, Mr. Oliphant read us a paper about some mysterious experience that he declared was the Baptism of the Holy Ghost, and was the birthright of everyone ; urging us to seek the experience for ourselves. I confess, with my nose for heresy and my experience of fanatics, I scented out what he meant ; but one of my friends did not, and she was profoundly impressed with the mysterious reference to some wonderful ' it ' that was to be the aim of our desires. When he closed the paper, she said in her sweet, childlike way, ' What would'st thou have me to do in order to gain this ? ' Immediately he coloured up to the roots of his hair, and said, ' I could not tell you in this company '. It flashed into my mind that if he had answered her what was really in his mind, he would have said, ' Come and get into bed with me '. However, nothing more was said then, and we separated for the night, but I was convinced from the behaviour of our hostess and her daughters that they had been more or less initiated into the mystic rites of this new religion. The next morning Mr. Oliphant asked for a private interview with me, in which he told me that he believed my husband was called to enter into and propagate the views he held, and he urged me to beg him not to stop short of the full consummation. I asked what the full consummation was. He said, ' You noticed the question that was asked me last night ? Do you know what I would have answered ? ' I did not tell him what I had thought, but asked him, ' What would you have answered ? ' His reply was, ' If I dared to I would have said, " Come and get into bed with me ".' I then proceeded to expostulate with him, though I might as well have talked to Niagara. I asked him if it were not possible to lead people into this glorious experience he spoke of without personal contact. He said no, it was not. ' But ', I said, ' are you not afraid, Mr. Oliphant, that some day some of these women will betray you, and you will get into a great deal of trouble ? ' He said yes, there was always that danger, but that the missionary who propagated a new faith, and especially such a splendid faith as the one that he had been propagating, must not hesitate at any risk, but must be willing to face martyrdom, if necessary, in the cause of truth. Nothing I said had the slightest effect, which is always true with fanatics, no matter how convincing one's arguments or how clear one's reasoning. They seem to be compelled to dree their weird, possessed by the idea that they have direct communication with God, and that therefore they are raised above the region of human argument or human reasoning.

I felt sure, as I left the house, that trouble was brewing for the hostess, who was evidently strongly under Oliphant's influence, and I was not surprised to hear shortly after that the husband had come home and turned Oliphant out of the house. How he managed to go through life without an open scandal, has always been a mystery to me, except that those whom he had deluded must have been too much ashamed of their delusions ever to speak of them. When his life was written by Mrs. Oliphant, the novelist, a cousin of his, I felt as if it was not right to have such a eulogy set forth of him

when all these things were behind the scenes, but I
concluded it was not my business to enlighten her,
and I felt sure she would never have believed it if I
had told her. He seemed, when you were with him,
the very last person for such things. He was a cultivated
gentleman of apparently a great deal of good worldly
sense, and, except to the initiated, conveyed no idea
of the inner secrets of his life. In this lay largely his
power over others, because when so cultured and
apparently sensible a man spoke in the veiled way in
which he did of some wonderful experience that had
transformed his life, one could hardly help but believe
that it must be an experience worth knowing and sharing.
In order to explain to me about the counterparts he drew
the picture of

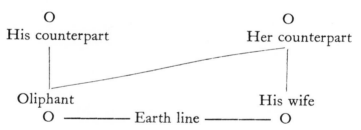

O   O
His counterpart   Her counterpart

Oliphant   His wife
O ———— Earth line ———— O

an earth line with two dots at quite a distance from
each other, one representing himself and the other his
wife. In a perpendicular line over each of these dots
he drew two others, the one over him represented his
counterpart, and the one over his wife represented her
counterpart. He told me that during his wife's life
they never came together as man and wife, but each

one had marital relations with their own counterparts. But the moment she died, she was united with her counterpart and the spiritual one came directly to him and dwelt within him. What his counterpart thought of this he omitted to tell me, but I have no doubt they all harmonized together.

Afterwards, when he married the second wife, I heard that he said he married her because whenever she was present he felt the presence of his first wife and her counterpart more strongly than he did at any other time. He assured me in the interview we had that I was not my husband's counterpart, but that he could find his counterpart if he would only pursue the path that Mr. Oliphant would mark out. He said that to find your counterpart was the consummation of human bliss, and that everybody in the world, if they knew what true happiness was, would give up every other pursuit and devote themselves to this search.

CHAPTER IX

MISS X.'S FANATICISM

MR. HARRIS has published a great many books containing the most marvellous and fantastic mystical revelations—which he declared at least were revelations. For instance, he described how a Father in this world who has an arch-natural counterpart has a little arch-natural child running about, and under some spiritual evolution which I don't exactly remember, the spiritual counterpart becomes involved in the earthly Father and then the child is swallowed up in this two in one, as he called this double Father and Mother. These books are being issued to this day. As regards Harris himself, I have heard that he was forced by public opinion to marry one of the women who was in his community, and that he has given up his life at his arch-natural house, and is living as an ordinary citizen in some Californian town.

I came to know a great deal about him and his teaching, through an especial friend of mine who was a very cultivated and charming lady in one of our large American cities. She had a yearning after spiritual things, but was in the midst of very worldly surroundings and had no help from anyone around her. At one time she crossed the ocean on the same vessel with Mr. Harris. She knew nothing about him, except that he struck her as being a very spiritually minded man, and she was deeply interested in conversations with him.

He almost convinced her during the voyage that her eager quest after truth could be best satisfied by joining his community. When she parted from him he told her that as soon as he had had the revelation that she was to come to them, he would communicate with her. Months passed and she heard nothing. At last, having become very hungry after spiritual things, she made up her mind to write to him to see if he could give her any help. He did not reply himself, but one of his disciples, Miss W., replied for him in a very beautiful letter in which she assured this lady that she could find all the help she needed if she would come to Mr. Harris's home at Brocton, New York. She went, and spent a week of great interest there. It seemed to her that she had at last found a resting-place for her soul, and she listened with intense interest to all that Miss W. told her of their views and their life. Mr. Harris himself was not there at the time, but was engaged in another town where he was carrying on a very success-ful business and making a great deal of money. Miss W. gradually divulged the fact that if this lady came to him, it would have to be on the condition of absolute obedience to ' Father ', as they called Mr. Harris. Miss X. was disinclined to make an unconditional promise, but said she would be willing to obey him entirely in everything that she felt was right ; but this Miss W. declared would not do ; it must be a promise of unconditional obedience whether the thing looked to her right or wrong. ' But ', said Miss X., ' what could he possibly tell us to do that would be wrong ? such a holy man as he is ? ' Miss W. replied that things often looked wrong to a person that was not very far on in the spiritual life, which to those who had advanced further were righteous.

Miss X. had no suspicion of anything in particular, but she could not bring her mind to the point of promising unconditional obedience to any human being, and Miss W. informed her sorrowfully that it was very evident she had not yet received the Divine call. She left Brocton with a heavy heart, almost afraid that she had closed the door of mercy to herself, and yet absolutely unable to make the required surrender.

In the course of their conversations, Miss W. had told her that there were two very dangerous Quakers in Philadelphia, Mr. and Mrs. Pearsall Smith, who had hindered some most important English disciples from joining the community. Miss X. did not know us at the time, though she had heard of us as religious teachers, and we had many mutual friends.

Her unrest of soul still continuing, she found herself constantly recurring to the thought of this mysterious, but fascinating, religion, and could not rid herself of the idea that there perhaps she would find that for which her soul longed. About this time she received quite a fortune, and in some way they must have heard of this at Brocton, for almost immediately she received another letter from Miss W. saying that ' Father ' believed that a renewed call had come from the Lord for her to join them. This meant, of course, that she was to take all her property and hand it over to Mr. Harris and throw herself into the community for life.

Then began a correspondence of the deepest interest to Miss X., by means of which she seemed to be irresistibly drawn to give up everything and take herself and all her property to join this community. In fact, she even went so far as to pack her trunks and make all her preparations to hand over her property, and started, fully expecting to find herself there.

I should say that during the course of this correspondence she had been assured over and over that God had reserved for her a wonderful destiny. She was to be made the ' Queen ' of the community, and was to have a career of great honour and glory. It was all presented in a most enticing guise, and she was warned over and over that it was her day of grace and that if she resisted this call dire misfortunes would follow. She was, as I said, all packed ready to go, but still felt some misgivings, and determined on the way through Philadelphia to see these dreadful people against whom Miss W. had warned her.

She wanted to know what arguments they had used to prevent the English friends spoken of from joining the community. We had a mutual friend who had also been nearly entrapped by this community ; and, on arriving at Philadelphia, she went direct to this friend and asked her to take her to see Mrs. Smith. They came one morning to our house, and in my little study we had a full conversation. At that time I knew little

about Mr. Harris's community, but I did know more
about the common sense of religion, and I pointed out
to Miss X. that it could not possibly be according to
the religion of Christ, as it was set forth in the Bible, that
any one human being should assume such absolute
authority over other human beings ; that the only
obedience to human authority which could be demanded
in religion was obedience *in the Lord,* which meant
that one could only do that which seemed to them
right in the eyes of God. I also pointed out that nowhere in the Bible were Christians told that it was to be
a universal demand that all their property should be
surrendered to another person ; that the instance
brought forward by Mr. Harris and his followers of
the young man being told to sell all and follow Christ
was an isolated instance, and could not possibly be
meant for universal application. I also said that where
there was so much mystery there must be something
that had to be hidden, and that to give oneself up to
unknown courses was the height of folly in a sensible
human being. I used, in short, the commonsense
arguments that would occur to any unbiased mind in
the face of such mysterious demands.

Somehow my arguments, combined with the confirma-
tion from the friend who had accompanied her and
who had herself been to Brocton, and who, without
actually knowing anything concerning Mr. Harris's
views, had felt an instinctive sense that something
was wrong—seemed to prick the bubble—and she
decided not to go. Some years passed, and then another

effort was made to draw her into the snare, and Mr. Oliphant was sent to see her, but made very little impression upon her. Still, a fresh link seemed to be made, and Miss W. began to write again most persuasive and enticing letters, and again induced her to visit the community.

Much more was told her at this second visit than had been told her before. The doctrine of counterparts was revealed to her, and she was told that God had a wonderful counterpart in waiting for her, whose life was incomplete until she joined him. She found that ' Father ' had a counterpart who was called ' Lily Queen ', and who was believed by the community to be the consoler and caretaker of every troubled soul that came to her ; but she discovered that the method of getting this consolation from Lily Queen was rather peculiar : The troubled soul was to go to Mr. Harris's room and get into bed with Lily Queen. ' But what became of Mr. Harris ? ' asked Miss X. ' Oh, Lily Queen is inside of Father, and consequently he, of course, stays in the bed, and by getting into his arms we get into her arms.'

In all this time she did not see Mr. Harris himself, but had intercourse only with Miss W. and the other members of the community. All this greatly shocked Miss X., and she left the community troubled and distressed, and yet still fascinated by the apparent real spiritual insight and wonderful self-abnegation of the devotees there.

After leaving, moreover, Miss W. continued to write

to her, sometimes three or four times a day, letters of the most solemn and impressive kind, urging her not to resist the 'Divine call', and to close with God's wonderful offers of grace and mercy while there was yet time. Moreover, she pointed out to her that the whole salvation of her family depended upon her faithfulness ; that while she resisted this Divine call, she was a direct barrier in the way of their spiritual advancement. All this so worked upon her feelings that she finally almost decided again to go, and this time did not consult anyone, feeling that the arguments used before could have no weight now.

She had, however, a very wise and devoted father to whom she confided the fact that she thought of taking all her property and joining this community. He was entirely ignorant of the whole line of teaching ; but, seeing how deeply concerned her soul was, he said : ' If you must go, daughter, I will not put a straw in your way, but I shall go with you ; and, if I can't enter the community, at least I shall live near to see that you are protected '. This made her hesitate, and some time passed, letters continually coming from Miss W., full of the most solemn adjurations and warnings. Finally there came a letter from another member of the community, marked ' confidential ', and opening with the imperative demand that she should not let the rest of the community know that the letter had been written. This letter was evidently written in order to add inducements to make her come, for it pictured forth the wonderful destiny that awaited her, the exalted position she was to have in the community, and the untold delights and joys that were to be her portion. It assured her that when she discovered who her counterpart was she would be overwhelmed with happiness, and would realize that a greater privilege had fallen to her share than ever had been known to mortal before. The letter said that all the preparations were made to give her the most triumphal welcome that could be conceived of, and that God had in store for her marvels of glory and of grace beyond all that she could conceive, and closed by saying that all this was a profound secret which had been told to the community, but which she was not to know of. But the writer thought that it would be a help to her to decide if she could know the blessings which awaited her, and had therefore written, but begged that her communications should be kept confidential.

This betrayal of the secrets of the community by one of its apparently most earnest members shocked Miss X.'s sense of honour so much that it made her doubt the reality of a religion that could allow its devoted followers to take such a course ; and somehow it seemed to break the spell once more and to deliver her afresh from the snares in which she had again become involved. She immediately wrote to Miss W. stating these facts, and enclosed the letter that had been sent her, and said she had finally decided to give the whole thing up. Of course this roused great animosity in the community, and letter after letter of vituperation followed, and the spell was for ever and completely broken. But a

day or two after this decision had been arrived at a letter
came, the first she had ever received, from Mr. Harris
himself, which, if she had received it before her decision,
she felt sure would entirely have altered everything.
It was exactly the sort of letter that would have entranced
her and made her feel that it was a ' call of God ' which
she would not dare to disobey. But by the time it came
the revulsion had become so great that it had no influence.
She found from its date that it should have arrived
several days before, but that in some mysterious way
it had been mislaid in the community and not forwarded
at the right time, and it seemed to her that if the letter
had been really of God, He would certainly have managed
that it should have come in time to accomplish its work ;
in fact, the spell was so completely broken that she
began to see the folly and the danger of the whole thing,
and was convinced that Mr. Harris's object had been
from the beginning to secure herself and her money
for his own uses.

She told me that the last she heard of Mr. Harris
was two or three years ago when by the force of public
opinion he had been obliged to give up his community
in California and marry Miss W., and had come to live
in New York. His wife, the former Miss W., had
been an inmate in a private hospital in which a friend
of Miss X.'s was also a patient. The matron of the
hospital told her that Mr. Harris had become a drivelling,
sensual old man ; that his only thought appeared to
be hugging and kissing women ; that he had tried to
do it to her and that she had to avoid ever being alone

with him. And she was convinced that his wife knew his weakness and tried to prevent his ever being alone with any woman. But she said that he met her one day in the hall when nobody was about, and that he rushed up to her and threw his arms around her and exclaimed, ' I love you ! I love you ! I love you ! You do not know how I love you ! ' And she was obliged to make her escape in order to avoid further demonstrations.

Miss X.'s search after spiritual things continued in spite of her disappointments, and I think it is safe to say that she tried to find satisfaction for her soul in every known form of religious belief, but failed in all. Finally, she was thrown in with Roman Catholics, was convinced of the true claims of that Church and joined them, and has from that moment had absolute peace and rest, with no further religious troubles of any kind, and is leading a most useful and happy life, working for the Lord in Roman Catholic ways. At present she is very much interested in the starting of a Roman Catholic College for girls in connexion with the Order of Notre Dame. To show what complete satisfaction her soul has found in this Church, she said to us after having joined it : ' Well, Robert and Hannah, I've tried religious quacks for a great many years and have never found any satisfaction from them, but now at last I have found, in our Church, spiritual teachers who have been trained by centuries of study and experience and are able to meet all the spiritual difficulties that beset any soul, and they give me satisfactory answers to every difficulty. I have no further troubles, and as regards doctrines, I feel that I, with my small experience and limited means of education in such subjects have no right to have any opinion ; but in our Church there is a body of men trained for this very purpose, and to them I leave the settling of all such questions.'

She has often assured me that if I would truly follow the light, I also would be brought into the Roman Catholic Church. Needless to say, that has not happened yet, but I can easily see that if one could once bring one's mind to believe that that Church was infallible, it *would* bring peace to give up all speculations and throw oneself blindfold into its arms.

CHAPTER X

DIVINE GUIDANCE

THE whole subject of Divine Guidance was to me
a very interesting one ; largely, no doubt, because
of my education in the Quaker Society. It naturally
seemed a beautiful idea to think that we could be directly
guided in all our affairs by the Almighty, and I was
ready to catch at any straw which seemed to promise
success. My idea of guidance in those days was of
having impressed upon my mind in some miraculous
way the will of God ; and the teaching I received was
that instant, unquestioning obedience to these impressions
was the only way to make the thing a certainty. The
old Friends, when I would object sometimes to certain
steps as appearing unreasonable and mistaken, would
always tell me that light was given for one step, and
that, as I obeyed the first step, light would be given
for the second : consequently the pathway looked like
a series of blind steps, each one taken without any
comprehension of where it would lead, but sure to lead
aright, the steps following one another in a Divine
order, unseen by myself, but planned by God.

I had an old Grandmother who was always telling
me these things, and urging me to take the first step
in obedience to my inward Guide. When I felt wicked,
I used to say to myself, ' Well, I will never take the

first step, because then I shall not have to take the second '. But when I felt pious I used to be eagerly on the look out for guidance in this first step. Among the Quakers this guidance was so well regulated that it never took the form of any extreme Fanaticism, but was mostly concerned with the subject of religious service, and of dress and reading and matters of daily life.

I had one friend who was greatly given up to this sort of guidance, and who told me that she hardly ever could get downstairs in the morning without feeling led to go back and change some article of dress for another less attractive, and that many a time she would run to a meeting with her fingers in her ears for fear she would have to go back and put on something conspicuous, as a cross for the benefit of her soul. The childhood and young girlhood of this friend were made miserable by this matter of what she considered guidance. She was very brilliant, and wrote a good deal—really good writing, I should judge from what she has since done—but she felt guided continually to destroy what she wrote, throwing the manuscripts into the fire as a supreme sacrifice to the Deity she was trying to serve. The fact was that in this theory of guidance all the things we liked best and enjoyed most were the things that we had to sacrifice, and we were almost afraid to acknowledge to ourselves that we enjoyed anything for fear that we should immediately feel led to give it all up. Of course, with healthy natures these ideas of guidance would not do much harm, although they might occasion, as they did to me, times of great perplexity ; but, with emotional and introspective natures the mischief was very great, and drove many to the verge of, and even in some cases, completely into insanity. I knew one of the Quaker preachers at the meeting that I attended who had got a new drawing-room carpet, and was so pleased with it that immediately she felt she must do something to mortify her pride, and felt ' led ' to have a load of stones and mud wheeled in and upset upon it. I remember that I always looked upon her with the most profound reverence, as having been one who had been specially favoured with Divine Guidance, and who had made a supreme sacrifice to obey it.

At one time in my experience, I also had a new carpet of which I was very proud because we were not very rich, and it was a great thing for us to get a new Brussels carpet. Shortly after the carpet was put down my husband felt drawn to have a number of rough working-men come every Sunday morning to this drawing-room for a Bible class. It was a great trial to me to have my carpet used in that way and I was inclined to resent it, but I knew as a Christian I ought not to feel so, and yet I did not exactly see how to overcome the feeling. Someone happened to say to me about that time that there was always some passage in Scripture which would help you out of every difficulty, and when I was praying about this difficulty of mine I said, ' Well, I am certain that there is no Scripture anywhere that says anything about drawing-room carpets ', and at that very moment there flashed into my

mind the passage, ' Take joyfully the spoiling of your
goods '. And I immediately seized hold of that word
of God as the Sword of the Spirit with which to conquer
my enemy, and from that moment I rather enjoyed
seeing these rough men tramp over my new carpet ;
and I may say in conclusion that that carpet seemed
as if it never would wear out. It lasted for years, until
I was tired and sick at the sight of it. But this was not
an instance of Guidance, but rather of plain Christian
duty.

I had another friend who found it difficult even to
get through her meals without being ' led ', just as
she was putting a mouthful to her lips, to feel that she
ought not to eat that mouthful. (This same young friend
I met in the days when I understood better myself.)
And when she would come to me in trouble as to what
she should eat or what she should wear, or where she
should go, I was obliged to give her a piece of advice,
to which I rather objected, which was, to ' ask Josiah '.
Josiah was her husband and I gathered from all she
said that he was a man of a good deal of good sense,
and although I did not as a general thing approve of
letting husbands decide things for their wives, I found
that in her case she had so many scruples that it was
almost a necessity.

She lived in a semi-detached house with a little green
in front, and in the middle of the green was a flower bed.
Her neighbour used to take turns with her every spring
in filling this bed with flowers. When it came to her
turn, she was greatly concerned about the colour of the

flowers, and especially felt led not to have red geraniums. But one spring her neighbour especially wanted her to have red geraniums, and she came to me in the greatest trouble to know what she was to do. Fortunately by this time I had a little sense, and I told her that I thought Heavenly Father would not have created red geraniums if it could possibly be wrong for anybody to have them, and this relieved her mind. She lived quite a way from my house and she would sometimes, in the midst of doing some sewing—for instance, making a dress for her little girl—get into such a snarl as to whether it would be right to put ten buttons or six down the back of the little child's dress, that she would have to drop everything and come down to me to ask me what she should do. I had enough sense by this time to know that there was no divine reality in the thing, consequently all I used to do was to try and find out what she really wanted, and then tell her to do that, so that I was a very comforting Father Confessor.

I had another friend who was fond of painting, and had several pictures which her family greatly prized, and who ' felt led ' one day to burn these pictures, and took them out into a field behind the house and made a bonfire of them, feeling that it was the supreme sacrifice she could offer. This was in the days when I was intensely interested in trying to learn all about the subject of guidance, and I remember that I looked upon this performance with the most reverential awe, and only wished that I could be moved to some similar sacrifice ; but for some reason I never seemed able to get any clear guidance, considerations of common sense always coming in to upset any approaches to what I considered might be guidance.

I knew a woman, who was one of the dearest and most earnest Christians in her circle, but who had given herself up to follow these impressions, honestly believing that they were the voice of God. She was visiting a friend, and was taken ill in this friend's house. One morning, when she was in bed, her friend came in to see her, and laid some money upon the dressing-table. She was called away suddenly, and left the money behind her. As soon as she was gone, an impression came to the invalid that the Lord wanted her to take that money in order to illustrate the truth of the text that ' all things are yours '. The impression was so strong that she got out of bed and took the money and hid it under her pillow. In a little while her friend came back to get the money. The poor invalid was afraid to tell her what she had done, and was reduced to the subterfuge of saying she thought somebody must have come in without her noticing and stolen it. A great deal of trouble ensued ; the lady of the house became suspicious, and the poor invalid began to become doubtful as to whether it had really been the Lord's voice or not, and underwent agonies of remorse. At last the lady of the house, from her prevarications and excuses, was convinced that the invalid had stolen it, and turned her out of the house, and it occasioned a permanent breach between them. What the invalid herself thought of it afterwards, I do not know, for I have never seen her since.

In spite of the difficulties which they so often involved, I felt sure that the true Divine Guidance must be the greatest possible blessing this world could hold, and during that summer in Coulter St., Germantown, of which I have spoken elsewhere, when that strange household lived next door to us, I made the most determined effort of my life to get at the secret of it. And it was in this wise. Among other striking and apparently holy characteristics, Mr. L. and the W.'s seemed to know all about the guidance of the Holy Spirit, and to experience it in a very wonderful way. They seemed, in fact, to have gained such a familiarity with the ' voice of the Lord ' as to live in constant communion with Him, and to have His guidance in all the smallest details of their lives—as to what they should wear, and what they should eat, and even as to what rooms they should occupy, and what chairs they should sit in, and, in fact, how they should order every moment of their lives. All this was intensely interesting and delightful to me, and I longed to know just such a life lived in the Lord's presence and guided and controlled by Him, and was never tired of hearing about it. I have described elsewhere how I tried and failed to live in the same way. From all my experience I have come to the conclusion that Divine Guidance is one of the most contagious things in the religious life, and that you are almost sure to catch the same sort of guidance as the people with whom you associate.

A striking illustration of this occurred during this same summer. The reputation of this household as

religious teachers had spread far and wide. Among
the many enquirers who came to be instructed by these
teachers were a great many saintly women, not all
young by any manner of means, and most of them with
a large amount of spiritual knowledge and experience,
and apparently a great deal of prudence and good sense.
But, strange to say, one after another of these dear,
sober, middle-aged sisters, many of them older than
Mr. L. himself, would in some mysterious way begin
to 'feel led' to give him a kiss, and in spite of all the
agony of mind they had to endure at the thought of
such an unwomanly and apparently immodest performance, they could find no peace until the sacrifice was
made, and the called for kiss bestowed, when floods of
joy and peace would fill their souls. As whispers about
these supreme sacrifices to duty spread through the
house, one and another caught the infection, and finally
it reached me. One day when I was alone reading
my Bible and praying for guidance (and however else
it may have been with the others, in my case it certainly
was only an honest longing to know the Lord and be
conformed to His likeness), suddenly, in the moment
of a most solemn act of consecration to God, a voice,
that seemed to be spoken in my inner consciousness
from a source entirely distinct from my own personality,
said plainly, ' If you want to be *entirely* consecrated to
God, you must kiss Mr. L.' I was horror-struck, and
my whole being revolted from such an action. But
what was I to do ? I had started out to follow the Lord
absolutely whithersoever He should lead me, and how

could I not believe that an inward voice which came to me at such a solemn moment, when I felt myself to be so especially in the Lord's presence, was a voice from Him ? There seemed nothing for me to do but to surrender my will in the matter and to say, ' Yes, Lord, if it is Thy will, repulsive as it is, I will do even this ! ' Perfect peace at once filled my heart, and I felt like a lamb led to the slaughter, and only awaiting the moment of sacrifice.

Fortunately, however, the impression passed from my mind, and for several days, although I was seeing Mr. L. continually, I never once thought of it when I was in his presence, though when I was away from him it weighed on me like a dreadful nightmare. One evening, however, when a little company of us had been sitting at his feet listening to his wonderful teachings, I was unexpectedly left alone with him for a few minutes, and the voice spoke again, ' Now you must do it '. But before I had hardly had time to hear the voice, Mr. L. broke the silence by saying, ' Mrs. Smith, if ever you should feel led to kiss me, don't do it, for you are not the sort of person to do such things '. I said nothing, and in a moment one of the family entered the room, and to my great relief and unspeakable thankfulness the whole impression passed away from my mind and never recurred again.

In looking back I cannot attribute the fact that I was preserved from thus making a fool of myself, while others, equally good, had been ensnared, to any special favour of God towards myself, and certainly not to any especial goodness on my part, but simply to the fact that I really was not, as Mr. L. said, ' that kind of person ', and that he had insight enough to see that even if I should have been betrayed in a moment of excitement into such an action, my substratum of common sense would sooner or later rise to the surface and make me a dangerous disciple.

Another instance of the contagion of so-called Divine Guidance occurred to me during this same summer. Miss W. had told me, as an instance of the wonderful way in which she was guided by the Lord, that when she had been at the dressmaker's a few days previously having a dress fitted, in the midst of the fitting the inward Voice told her to kiss the dressmaker. She said she had at once obeyed, with the result that the dressmaker had burst into tears and said that no one had kissed her since her mother's death some years before. And, Miss W. said, it had so touched the dressmaker's heart that she received with thankfulness the ' message from the Lord ' that Miss W. felt then led to give her. I was deeply interested in this recital, and thought, with almost a feeling of envy, how beautiful it must be to be so guided, but never supposed for a moment that any such guidance could ever be granted to me. The incident, however, passed out of my mind and when, a few days afterwards, I went to my dressmaker, who happened to be the same as Miss W.'s, I had entirely forgotten the whole matter. But suddenly, as I was in the midst of having my dress tried on, it all came back to me, and an inward Voice told me I too must kiss the dressmaker. I was rather set back by this, for it seemed to me a most awkward and distasteful performance, probably quite as awkward and distasteful to the poor dressmaker as to myself. However, as I was honestly trying to be obedient to the inward voice, I dared not refuse, and said to the dressmaker, ' The Lord tells me to kiss you ', and proceeded to bestow a kiss upon her cheek. I must say the whole thing fell very flat. The poor woman coloured crimson with embarrassment, and I shared her embarrassment. No tears followed, and no ' message from the Lord ' came either to her or to me. She hurried to finish her fitting and I hurried to leave the house, thankful to get alone where I could endure my mortification in silence. I could not understand why my obedience to the inward Voice failed to produce the same results as in the case of Miss W., but concluded it was because she was more holy than I. I told a very dear friend, who was a great believer in Divine Guidance, all about it, and a few days afterwards she came to me with the story that she too, when at the same dressmaker's the next day after I had told her of my experience, had had the same interior voice telling her that she too must kiss the dressmaker. Like me, she had been afraid to refuse, and had given the poor dressmaker the third kiss from the Lord. In her case also it fell quite flat, and they quickly separated, overwhelmed with mutual embarrassment. What the poor dressmaker thought I never knew, as my friend and I were too much mortified ever to go to her again. But, when my friend had finished her story, a sudden illumination came to me, and I said, ' Sister Sarah, this whole thing is catching. I caught it from Miss W., and you caught it from me. Now we must put a stop to it, and not tell another human being about it, or we shall have every one of our friends kissing their dressmakers, and making fools of themselves all round'. My friend agreed to speak of the subject to no one, and I never heard of any more dressmakers being kissed.

Out of all my own personal experiences as to Divine Guidance I found at last that *my* guidance mostly came in very commonplace ways, and chiefly through impulses of kindness or courtesy. Nearly always when I did things purely to oblige people or to be kind to them, without any especial thought of guidance, they were very apt to turn out to have been the most direct guidance possible and to have led to quite remarkable results. This was especially the case with regard to my book, 'The Christian's Secret of a Happy Life'. It was written simply and only to oblige my husband, who was editing a monthly religious paper at the time, and who begged me each month for an article. I had no feeling whatever of being ' called ' to write it, nor that I was being ' guided ' in any way. The recent Women's Crusade Movement in America had thoroughly awakened me to the need of temperance reform, and I had joined their ranks. My husband in coming to England had been ordered by his doctor to take wine at dinner. I did not myself believe that it did him the least bit of good, and it was a great trial to see him taking it. Consequently, I made his giving it up the condition of my writing an article. I said, however, that I would only write one, and that he need not expect me to continue. For some reason, however, my article excited more interest than anything else in the paper, and he begged me so much to go on writing that I finally consented to give him an article every month. But these articles were dragged from me, so to speak, at the point of the bayonet, for I never wrote them in any month until the printers were clamouring for their copy. I could not be said, therefore, to have had any great feeling or sense of being called to write them, beyond the fact that I did it to oblige my husband, and yet these articles, collected in a book, made the 'Christian's Secret of a Happy Life,' which book has been translated into almost every language in the world, has gone through a hundred editions, and very few books on experimental religion seem to have been as helpful to God's children as this has been. I never go to a meeting that one or more persons do not tell me that that book is their principal guide in life, that they keep it under their pillows or beside their bed, and that in every spiritual emergency they go to it for help. I have thousands of letters telling of the blessing it has been and the many remarkable circumstances connected with it, which, if I had time to look over my papers, I could insert. It has been the turning-point in thousands of lives, and yet it contains no deep mysteries, and is in reality the simplest, most commonplace statement of a few fundamental religious principles, which, however, are of universal application. I speak of all this especially on account of the fact that the book was not written under any special feeling of being called to write it, nor with any idea that it was in the least an especially religious service. I did it simply and only to oblige my husband, and that was all there was to it. I didn't even pray much about it, nor had I any thought that I was doing a work for the Lord ; and, as I have had many similar experiences in my life, I have come to the conclusion that an ordinary everyday walking in the path of duty, and especially in the path of kindness, is a better foundation for doing good work for the Lord than any great ecstacies of inspiration, or any special sense of having a ' mission ' or being ' called ' to a special service. The fact is most of my work which has been most successful has been done purely from motives of kindness and courtesy. I have found this to be the largest factor in the guidance of my life.

On one occasion I had a dear friend who was very nervous. She used to cry on the smallest provocation and about things which had no personal element in them, except that they upset her nerves. For instance, she said that if she was going along the street, and some one who was going in the same direction suddenly turned round and faced her, she would burst into tears ; or, if she saw anyone who was particularly ugly, or who had any specially disagreeable feature or tone of voice, it would upset her nerves, and put her all in a quiver of distress. She and I attended a little prayer meeting that was held once a week at a friend's house, where we went more intimately into our own personal experi-

ences than could have been done in a public meeting.
One morning she announced to us at the beginning of
the meeting that we were to devote that meeting to her ;
she told us about her nervousness and said, ' I do not
think that a Christian woman ought to be so much
upset by trifles, and I want you all to unite with me
in prayer at this meeting that I may be delivered.' I
confess that I had not much expectation that praying
would do her any good, as I thought it was a physical
condition which probably could never be alleviated.
But when the time came we all knelt down to pray,
and of course I knelt with them. I supposed that there
would be fervent prayers offered for our friend by the
others, and I did not really intend to pray myself at all,
but to my astonishment the whole little company prayed
all round in turns and never mentioned her case. It
seemed to me that this was very impolite, and, in fact,
unkind, when she had thrown herself so upon our
sympathy, and so mainly, with the idea that she might
not be disappointed, and simply out of an impulse of
politeness and kindness, when the rest had finished
I prayed for her ; but, I confess, I had not the slightest
idea that anything would come of it, except that her
feelings would be smoothed by the recognition of her
need. Imagine my astonishment when we rose from
our knees and she turned to me and said, ' Hannah,
thy prayer is answered ; I am cured '. And as a fact
she was cured from that time.

Another case was once when I was attending a meeting
After I had spoken, a woman rose from the middle of

the meeting and said, ' If that lady who has just spoken
will come and lay hands on me and pray for my recovery
I shall be healed of a throat trouble that has caused me
great suffering for many years, and for which the doctors
declare they can do nothing.' I thought to myself,
' How little that woman knows how unbelieving I am
with regard to faith healing. I am certain my prayers
would do her no good.' And, in fact, I was rather
amused at her ignorance, and had to cover my face to
hide a smile. The meeting went on for a little longer,
and by the time it closed I had entirely forgotten the
incident, and began to talk to a friend beside me, when
someone came hastily in and said, ' Mrs. Smith, that
woman is waiting for you to come and pray for her,
and you must come at once, for she says her throat is
very bad.' Out of kindness I went, but I said to the
woman as I entered the room, ' You have sent for me
to pray for you, but I haven't a particle of faith that it
will do the least bit of good.' ' Yes, it will,' she replied ;
' it will cure me. Kneel right down here beside me,
and lay your hand on my throat and ask God to heal me,
and I know I shall be healed.' Out of kindness I did
as she wished, although I confess it seemed to me
something of a farce. However, when we rose from
our knees, to my amazement her voice was changed,
and she declared her throat was cured. I heard from
her quite often afterwards, and the story was always
the same, that the cure was complete.

As I bade the woman farewell, she said, ' Now,
Mrs. Smith, you have the gift of healing, and you

ought to exercise it.' I did not think it was likely to be true, but I thought I would try it, so I went to my sister, who was suffering from a chronic disease, told her the incident, and said, 'Now I am going to pray for thee, and if thee is cured I shall be sure I have the gift. If thee is not cured, then I shall think it was the woman's own faith that did it, and not my prayers.' There was no change in my sister's condition, so I came to the conclusion that I did not have the gift.

Another instance where the impulse of kindness produced wonderful results, was in the case of a friend who had become, from severe rheumatic suffering, a victim of the opium habit. One day when we were talking together, she said, ' I believe if you would pray for me, I could be cured of this habit.' I myself had no idea that it could be done, but, of course, when a person wanted me to pray for them, I should not think of refusing, so I kneeled down beside her wheel-chair and prayed, and the result in her case also was a complete cure.

This, and many similar instances, convinced me that one had only to do the kind thing which came nearest to hand, and one was pretty sure to be following the guidance of the Lord. It seems to me to illustrate the fact announced by our Lord when he said ' the Sabbath was made for man, and not man for the Sabbath ', meaning, as I believe, that religion was made to fit into man as he is in this world, and that to be a good human being is to be the best Christian that can be made. It is like a little girl I heard of once who was asked if she knew what it was to be a Christian, and she said, ' Yes, it's to do just as Jesus Christ would have done if he had been a little girl and lived in my house '. I feel more and more that it is a great mistake to think religion is something mysterious and out of the common order, and I am sure that while we are on this earth the highest we can attain to is to be the best human beings possible, and not try to be angels. When the butterfly is in the caterpillar stage of its existence, all it is called upon to do is to be a good caterpillar, and not try to stretch out wings that it hasn't got. When it becomes a butterfly, then it must cease to be a caterpillar and be a good butterfly. And we, when we leave this cocoon of ours, may then stretch our wings which we shall then have, but should not strain ourselves while in this cocoon to put out wings that we have not got. Religion is made for man : man as he is here and now ; and to be a good man or woman seems to me of far more account than to have the greatest possible ecstacy or to live in the greatest spiritual absorption. It is perfectly plain that God has put us into this world to be human beings, not angels, and his own teaching is that in that calling wherein we are called, there to abide. I am convinced that a large majority of the spiritual difficulties and the grave spiritual mistakes made by Christians arise from the fact that they are trying to be something that they were never meant to be, and to live on a plane that they were not meant to enter until they leave this world. All the fanaticisms of which I give an account in this record distinctly came from this cause. The dear Saints who fell into them were trying to be more than human. They tried to enter a region of which they knew nothing, and where they were therefore certain to be deceived.

CHAPTER XI

CONCLUSION

ONE of the most common delusions of fanaticism is that the leaders prominent in any special way come, sooner or later, to believe that they are Christs. Why this is I have never been able to discover, and, to tell the truth, I have never investigated this particular form of heresy very closely, because my common sense revolted from it at the start. Mr. L., however, the account of whose religious vagaries I have given in another place, not only believed that he was Christ, but thought that he was destined to be the father of ' Christ's children ', who were to found a race that was to revolutionise the world. These children, according to him, were to be begotten in a spiritual way, without bodily contact, but his practice did not bear out his assumption. Another Christ is alive at the present moment, and his name is J. Pigott, and the account of his fanaticism has been spread through the newspapers and is well known.

There is another Christ in Persia who has managed to get hold of some friends of my own. He lives in Akka, a military station in the northern part of Palestine. His name is Beha-Ullah. He and his followers are disciples of Bab, the well-known Persian religious leader. The Bab in his writings referred continually to a coming Great One, ' He whom God would manifest.' He constantly exhorted his followers not to reject this Great One when he should appear, and Beha-Ullah is supposed to be the realisation of this prophecy.

My own knowledge of this movement comes from two or three personal friends in England, who have become his disciples, and believe fully that he is, as he declares, a reincarnation of Christ, and that his religion is (they pretend) flooding the Eastern countries with new life and light. The sister of one of these friends came to me in great trouble because she was afraid that if she refused to become a disciple of Beha-Ullah she might be rejecting a real incarnation of Christ, and as I had helped her sometimes in her spiritual life, she came to me for advice. She was an earnest soul whose only desire was to know the truth. I frankly told her that I did not believe Beha-Ullah was any more Christ than I was, and that at that moment I knew a dozen Christs scattered around the suburbs of London.

There are a number of other delusions which are more obviously fanatical than those arising from Divine Guidance, and against which it is therefore not quite so necessary that Christians should be warned. The fanaticism of speaking with tongues is one of them. In this fanaticism it is believed that the Lord takes hold of your vocal organs and prays through you in new tongues. I do not know why it is that this delusion is so apt to come to Revivals, but I have known a great many instances, and in one case it went so far that two apparently sensible people allowed their young daughter of thirteen years to go out to China (I believe it was) as a missionary, she not knowing a word of Chinese, but being led to speak gibberish in this way, and they all believed that when she got there the Chinese would at once understand. What really happened when she did get there, however, I have never heard, but I presume she had to come home again.

The expectation of the Second Coming and of the End of the World is another very common form of fanaticism. I knew a party once who went out on a certain day all dressed up in white to a hill near the place they lived, expecting to be lifted up to the heavens. They hadn't ordered in any food, nor any winter clothes nor stores—they were so sure the end of the world was coming. Of course they had to do all this when they got back from the hill. But one of the curious things about it is that they were not the least discouraged, or seemed not to be at the time. I have noticed that this is generally the way with fanatics : they find some way of explaining their disappointments, and go on as before, and I believe it is because they are not in any sense led by reason, and so do not feel a need for their experiences to follow any logical plan.

Visions of the Lord, interior voices, conviction of sinlessness, belief in spiritual bodies are all more or less similar forms of fanaticism. I remember once I was introduced to a mysterious creature, a man he looked like, who was, I heard, of a strange sect called the ' Temple ', and who declared to me that he had not slept a wink for eight years, but had every night got out of his body and travelled around the world on errands of service for the Lord ! He declared that he saw angels as plainly as he saw men, and knew them all apart, and that Michael had light flaxen hair and Gabriel dark eyes and hair, and they all lived in the sun ! He was like all other cranks, with some slight variations, and like all the rest believed that his religion and his experiences were the ushering in of a new era in the world's history. I do not know how many ' new eras ' I have heard tell of. At least fifty, I should think, but they do not seem to have made any great difference to anyone but the poor souls who believed in them.

Spiritualism has always seemed to me a very dangerous path, which might at any minute lead to fanaticism, and for my own part I have found it necessary to rap every spirit that came over the head to find out whether it had any common sense before I surrendered myself to its guidance. Certainly, if there is any truth in the teaching of spiritualists it is clear that the spirit world must be inhabited by evil spirits as well as good, and there is an awful risk in giving oneself up to their control.

With Faith Healing I have had a great deal of experience, and I will record what I have found out about it. My first knowledge in regard to it came from Dr. C. of Boston, a most delightful Christian doctor, who thought he had discovered in the course of his practice that spiritual remedies for diseases were far more effectual than medical remedies, and consequently he combined with his ordinary medical treatment, treatment by prayer for those who desired it.

CONCLUSION

I heard of a great many cures by Dr. C., and finally I invited thirty invalids whom I knew to meet him at our house for him to pray with them, and, if possible, to heal them. He held a little meeting with them and pointed out that their faith must be added to his faith or nothing could be done, and he induced each one of that thirty to express the faith that they were healed, but I am sorry to say that as far as my knowledge went not a single one found any difference. Against this, I must put the fact that there were remarkable healings of nervous disorders, which, however, one could easily understand would be affected by a change of mind. Dr. C. was not the only faith healer whom I knew. I knew also a Mr. S. of New York, of whom wonderful stories were told, some of which I knew personally to be true. I have also met a great many individuals who have been cured, as they believed, by faith, and also I have known a great deal about Christian Science or the Mind Cure system of healing, and I believe I have investigated every phase of this kind of thing : Faith Cure, Divine Healing, Mental Science, Christian Science, Mind Cure, and I will tell you a story that I think will illustrate them all.

Four blind men were taken to see an elephant, and on their return were asked to describe it. One of the men was put at the elephant's trunk, one at his tail, one at his leg, and one at his ears. The description of the man who was put at the trunk was that an elephant was like a snake ; the man at the leg declared that an elephant was like the trunk of a tree ; the man at the ears declared that an elephant was like a palm-leaf ; and the man at the tail declared that an elephant was like a whip. Each man was right in the description of what he had seen, but none had seen the whole. My own impression is that all these different phases of faith cure, mind cure, etc., show us people getting at one especial feature of a grand truth, but that none of us yet have seen the whole. As far as I can make out this grand truth is the great fact that Spirit controls matter, and that if we were spiritually enough developed we should be able to control matter according to our measure as God does in His measure. I believe it is a Divine law that if we could say with absolute faith to a mountain, ' Be thou removed and be thou cast into the sea', the mountain would *have* to go. And I feel sure that all these different phases are efforts made towards this end, but that each one, because of our present undeveloped condition is weak and imperfect and liable to fail.

All doctors say that there is no more certain way of catching a disease than being afraid of it ; and equally no more certain way of being preserved from a disease than to have no fear. A desponding person is apt to fail in everything he undertakes, while a cheerful, courageous person seems to succeed without any effort. Our mental conditions are far more powerful to affect material things than we know, and I believe that there is here a secret for enormous power, if human beings once understood it. I was once talking with an occultist who had been through all the phases of occult teaching in India. He told me that there was one especial secret by which they lived, and by means of which they accomplished all their ends. I asked him to tell me that secret ; he said it would not be safe to tell it to anyone who had not been trained to use it aright, that if a mighty power such as it was were to be let loose in the world it would become, in the hands of unscrupulous or ignorant people, a fearful danger. He said it required long training and much discipline to make a person fit to receive the revelation of this secret. I made up my mind that if I possibly could I would entrap him into letting it out, and I skilfully led the conversation in such directions as I thought would conduce to this end. I asked him, among other things, to show me the occult treasures he possessed, thinking that in one of these I might perhaps discover his secret. Among other things, he brought out a very exquisite old volume of occult lore which he told me was exceedingly rare and difficult to procure, and he believed he was the only person in America who possessed a copy. I asked him how he got it. He said, ' I made up my mind to have it '. ' But ', I said, ' how could that procure it for you ? ' ' All things ', he said, ' come to him who knows how to will and to be silent', and then in a sudden burst of confidence he exclaimed, ' There, Mrs. Smith, that is the secret if you can understand it '.

It may be that all the mysteries of mesmerism and hypnotism can be explained in this way ; I think it is likely that some day it will be seen that we are able to be real co-workers with God in a sense far beyond what we have yet imagined. I believe that all the laws of life are the same, whether in the spiritual or the material world, and that what have seemed to us like miracles are really the outcome of laws about which we are ignorant, or into which we have only a scant insight. I cannot help thinking that prayer belongs to a region of law which we have not yet discovered. It is not that we change God's mind and induce Him by our coaxing to do something that He did not intend to do before ; but it is that our prayer has put us into line with His laws and made it possible for His law to work through our instrumentality. In prayer, all the Divine supply is provided, but it will not reach us unless we make the connexion that renders it possible for that supply to reach us. Our prayer neither creates the power nor coaxes it to come, but brings it by a Divine law to its destined end. To my mind there is an enormous amount of unbelief in the praying habits of Christians. It is as if God were unwilling to bestow blessings, and that it was necessary to go through great wrestlings and agonies in order to get them from Him. I think that story of Jacob and the Angel has done a great deal to perpetuate this attitude of mind. The careless reader supposes that it was Jacob who wrestled with the Angel and conquered the Angel by superior strength. But the real truth is that it was the Angel who wrestled with Jacob, that Jacob was the one who had to be conquered, not the Angel, and that the victory was only won when Jacob was made so lame and weak that he could not wrestle any longer. I believe that most of the conflicts and wrestlings of Christians are caused by their resistance to God, and that the victory comes only when they are too weak to resist any longer and are forced, as Jacob was, to submit. The sum of all my investigations is to be found in this, that there is a truth behind every form of Faith-healing, or Divine Healing, or Christian Science ; but at the same time I have come to the conclusion that faith and mind cure both lead sooner or later into spiritualism, and that they are therefore very dangerous.

But from all my investigations into Fanaticism, I did discover one truth, more important to Christians than any warnings about dangers in this world, and more fundamental than everything else in the world put together, and that truth was God. How I discovered it I have partly told in the preceding chapters and partly in other places, but I must tell it again.

I find in my ' Journal ', under date of June 13th, 1879, the following entry concerning the summer when the L. household lived next door to me :

' The Lord has been teaching me very blessed lessons about the interior life during the past six months. He sent some of His children to spend the summer in a house near ours. One of them especially helpful to me. She is what I call a " mystic "—one of those who know the Spirit's voice, and who walk alone with God. And she has taught me that the great thing in religion is to live and move and have our being in God. Not in experiences, nor in views, nor in doctrines, nor in anything of any kind, but simply in *God alone*. At last I

267

begin to understand what this means, and I believe I am beginning to live it.

'From this time onward God is to be all in all to me. I will acknowledge Him first in everything. . . . Definitely and forever I consent now to die as to any recognised self-life. It shall be henceforth no more I, but Christ.'

Under date of December of the same year I find the following entry :

'A grievous disappointment has come to me concerning the dear " mystics " who spent the summer near us. I have discovered that they are involved in frightful fanaticism and I am all perplexed and distressed as to the teaching concerning the interior life which I had received from them. I know the truth about it must exist, but if they have tried so faithfully to find it, and have been deluded, what hope have I of having any better success. Perhaps it is better not to try to live this interior life at all, but just to be an ordinary good human being, seeking to serve God in one's daily life, and being content to know but little of the inward voice, or of the conscious presence of the Holy Spirit. I confess I am sorely perplexed.'

This was almost the last entry in the Diary which I had kept at intervals for over forty years from the time I was seventeen, and which had been mostly a record of my spiritual life. It is not to be wondered at that I was, as I wrote, 'sorely perplexed'. But in spite of it all I *had* gained from this summer's experience a knowledge of God that enabled me to trust Him even through this sore perplexity, and that carried me triumphantly over it, and brought me into a peaceful resting in Him that has never been seriously disturbed since. The fact that I wrote no more in my Diary bears witness to this, for my Diary had always been more the refuge of my soul in all spiritual emergencies than anything else, and now that these emergencies were ended there seemed no occasion to make any farther entries. From that time I can truly say that my soul has rested absolutely in God, in God Himself, not in His promises, but in His character, not in what He has done or is doing, but in what He is. That God exists has been from that time enough for me, and I ask nothing more ; for, in the fact of His existence is shut up the fact that all is well for me and for the universe. It may seem strange that such an acquaintance with God could have come to me out of such a hotbed of fanaticism, but there is the fact, and there is no getting around it. Whatever else these dear deluded fanatics may have been or have done they did live in the presence of God in a most unusual sense, and did compel everyone who came to them for teaching to see God everywhere and in everything. And so effectually had they succeeded in establishing my soul in this habit that when the crash came and their fanaticism was revealed to me, instead of it driving me off from God it only made me cling all the closer to Him, and realize that though all human teachers might fail God was the same yesterday, to-day and for ever. He was enough for me and for the universe.

This was, as far as I can recollect, the last fanaticism

in which I made any explorations. I seemed somehow to have got behind the scenes and found out the way it was worked and I became convinced that all these strange manifestations and revelations were of the flesh, and belonged entirely to the physical parts of our nature, and that pure religion and undefiled was altogether apart from them, and resided not in the region of the emotions, but in the region of the will. ' Pure religion ', says Fénelon, 'resides in the will alone'. And again, ' the will to love God is the whole of religion '. I endorse these sayings with all my heart and am thankful beyond words that out of all my feverish search for emotional religion I was brought at last to see that a quiet steadfast holding of the human will to the will of God and a peaceful resting in His love and care is of infinitely greater value in the religious life than the most intense emotions or the most wonderful ' experiences ' that have ever been known by the greatest ' mystic ' of them all.

INDEX

'Moral Physiology,' by R. D. Owen, 98
Moravians, 34, 35
Mormonism, 57, 61
Mount Temple, Lord, 13
Muckers, the, 57
Müller, Bernhard, 36, 37

NAPIER, John, 52
Nashoba, Tennessee, 69, 70
Nauvoo, 84, 85
Nettleton's Revival, 51
New Divinity Party, 25
New Harmony, 67 ff.
New York, Puritans in, 22
Newton, Isaac, 52
Nothingarians, 73, 78
Noyes, John Humphrey, 56, 100 ff., 118, 123

OLIPHANT, Alice, 219 ff.
Oliphant, Laurence, 16, 17, 128 ff., 163, 219 ff., 234
Oneida Community, 56, 104 ff.
Owen, Robert, 35, 66, 68, 70, 87
Owen, Robert Dale, 70, 97
Owen, Rosamund, 98, 139, 223, 224

PAULINE Church, 102
Peace Union Settlement, 86
Pennsylvania, community in, 23, 35
Perfectionists of Oneida, 100 ff.
Persecution, religious, 23
Phalanxes, 77 ff.
Pilgrim Fathers, 22
Polish Community, in America, 85
Prince, Henry, 57
Puritans, 22
Purnell, David and Mary, 149, 150
Purple Mother, 98
Putney Community, Vermont, 102, 103

QUAKERS, 22, 37, 203, 240

R., Dr., 167
Rappites, 35, 66
Ripley, George, 63
Rock, Johann, 39
Ruskin Commonwealths, 86
Russell, Pastor T. C., 52
Russian sects, in America, 85